A GUID
THE MASONIC
TREASURER

PAUL SPARKS

Lewis Masonic

Cover image: Treasurer's Collar jewel of John Mott Thearle, 1856. *The Library and Museum of Freemasonry, London*

First published 2014

ISBN 978 0 85318 482 9

Published by Lewis Masonic
An imprint of Ian Allan Publishing Ltd, Hersham, Surrey KT12 4RG.

Printed in England

Visit the Lewis Masonic website at www.lewismasonic.co.uk

CONTENTS

ABOUT PAUL SPARKS

I completed a foundation course in accountancy in 1991, qualified as a Chartered Certified Accountant in 1995 at the age of 23 and then qualified as a Chartered accountant in 2009. I worked for local accountancy practices within Northamptonshire since 1991 and I became a partner in my current practice in 2009.

I was initiated to Dr. Field Lodge 8158 in November 2001 and was installed into the chair of King Solomon in 2006 and then again in 2011. In that same year, I was requested to cover the role of the Treasurer for the Province of Northants & Hunts following the former Treasurer's resignation. I continued to cover this role until my first provincial appointment to Acting Provincial Senior Grand Deacon in 2012. I have also been involved with the financial aspects of the Provincial headquarters following their relocation, and I was rewarded in 2013 with the promotion of Past Provincial Junior Grand Warden in recognition of my contribution.

I am also a founder member of a new special interest Lodge based around motor sport and the village of Silverstone in Northampton and I was appointed as the first Secretary of the Silverstone Lodge 9877 at its consecration in May 2013.

DEDICATION FROM PROVINCIAL GRAND MASTER OF NORTHAMPTONSHIRE AND HUNTINGDONSHIRE

It is with much pleasure that I commend the contents of this book to you. The position of Treasurer in any Lodge can be difficult at times and can be particularly difficult when taking this role for the first time, so it is with every confidence this book will be a great source of information to assist in that office.

R.W. Bro. Max Bayes,

PROVINCIAL GRAND MASTER,
PROVINCE OF NORTHAMPTONSHIRE AND HUNTINGDONSHIRE

PREFACE

This book is geared for those with little accountancy or bookkeeping experience, who are looking to either take on, or have recently been appointed to, the office of Lodge Treasurer - a task that may appear daunting, especially to those who have never carried out the office before.

It is one of the few offices in the Lodge, which has detailed rules laid down in the Book of Constitutions from United Grand Lodge of England, which I have used as a reference, and is presented to each new Mason after his Initiation. The role also has specific responsibilities from a financial aspect to the rest of the Lodge members. I hope that by following the simple steps in this handbook, you will have the basics to get you started.

I have used worked examples throughout this book and have then provided blank templates to follow for reference.

This book is also useful for those who will be Lodge Auditors as I have included a template of questions to ask when appointed to the office. It also gives some useful tips regarding some of the typical tax issues, which a Lodge Treasurer may come across.

P. A. Sparks

CHAPTER 1

THE LODGE TREASURER – AN OVERVIEW

Many people would never dream of taking on the role of a Lodge Treasurer, feeling that it is an office within the Lodge always meant for an accountant or bank manager. The purpose of this book is to try to dispel that myth. Before being initiated into my own Lodge, I met with various Past Masters of what was to become my Mother Lodge. During the meeting the question of my profession came up, to which I replied, I was an accountant. The response to my answer was, well I presume you will become the Treasurer at some point. Now, as a qualified accountant with many years' experience in public practice, this has never fazed me. The thought of taking this office within the Lodge seemed easy enough. Once I had progressed through the chair, it was the natural progression for me. I became Treasurer of my lodge in 2008.

Even with all my training for my professional exams and practical experience, I still did not know what exactly was required. I looked at accounts from the various lodges I visited. I read books, undertook research, and filled in the gaps from my own experiences. I needed to understand what should be done and why, rather than blindly following what had been done before.

The main guidance on being a lodge treasurer is from the Book of Constitution rule 153.

(a) "Save where a payment is made direct into the bank account of the Lodge, all moneys due to, or held for, the Lodge shall be paid or remitted, to the Treasurer direct, who shall without undue delay deposit the same in an account in the name of the Lodge at a bank to be approved by the resolution of the Lodge. The Lodge may by resolution authorise the Treasurer, but on no pretence any other Brother, to make payments from the Lodge's account by electronic means; in the absence of any such resolution all payments from the Lodge funds shall be made by cash or by cheque."

(b) "The Treasurer, if available to do so, shall make such payments as are duly authorised, or have been sanctioned by the Lodge. All cheques must bear the signature of two members authorised by the Lodge, of whom one shall, unless it is impracticable, be the Treasurer."

(c) "The Treasurer shall regularly enter a complete record of all moneys passing through his hands in the proper books of account, which shall be the property of the Lodge, and which, together with all Lodge funds and property in his possession, shall be transferred to his successor upon investiture. He shall prepare a statement of accounts annually at a date to be determined by the members, showing the exact financial position of the Lodge, which statement shall be verified and audited by a Committee of members of the Lodge annually elected for that purpose."

(d) "Copies of the accounts and of the certificate signed by the Audit Committee that all balances have been checked and that the accounts have been duly audited shall be sent to all members of the Lodge together with the summons convening the meeting at which they are to be considered. Such meeting shall be not later than the third after the date to which the accounts are made up. The books of account shall be produced for inspection in open Lodge at such meeting, and on any other occasion if required by a resolution of the Lodge."

(e) "The same procedure of annual accounts, audit and presentation to members of the Lodge, mutatis mutandis, be followed in relation to any funds maintained by or in connection with the Lodge (whether by the Treasurer or by a Charity or other Steward or by any other member of the Lodge) such as, but not limited to, a Lodge Benevolent Fund, the funds of a Charity or Benevolent Association, Dining Fund, Charity Box collections or other moneys receivable from individual members of the Lodge or any of its Officers."[1]

With this as the guidance from the "book that will set you right", it seems being a Lodge Treasurer can be a daunting task. This is why many Brethren, new to the office, are happy to follow what has always been done before. In order to start to elaborate on the role of a Lodge Treasurer I have interpreted the above wording as follows:

(a) With the proposed scrapping of cheques there may come a time when all Lodge subscriptions are paid to the Treasurer by electronic means. This will then take away some of the requirement to have all monies paid over without undue delay. The term of undue delay, is not defined within the Book of Constitutions, and therefore common sense should be applied. Any monies received should be paid into a bank account,

---

1   Book of Constitutions, United Grand Lodge of England ©2013

which bears the name of the Lodge. Historically, this will be the bank account set up by a previous Treasurer. However, if the new Treasurer believes it would be more convenient for him to change banks then this can be done. However, it will need to be proposed in open Lodge and voted on by a resolution. This will ensure that it is documented in the minutes by the secretary and as well as approved by all Lodge members. Again, with the advent of electronic banking, the Treasurer may be authorised by the Lodge to make electronic payments on behalf of the Lodge. This again must be done by a resolution to ensure that it is voted and approved by all members of the Lodge.

(b) The Treasurer can settle the normal Lodge Administration costs by cheque or by electronic means if approved. If cheques are used, they will need to be counter signed by another approved member of the Lodge. It should never be the case that a second cheque signatory just signs blank cheques, as this renders useless the control in place to ensure that the expenditure is in fact authorised. It may seem that this part of the rule contradicts the previous part (that only one person is required for electronic payments, but two approvals are required for a cheque). It is for this reason, that if electronic payments are to be made, they need to be authorised by the Lodge allowing the practice to be adopted. If electronic payments are not agreed then either cheque or cash payments would be the only recognised method for settling costs. For any costs, which are not part of the normal lodge expenditure, these will have to be voted on by resolution in open lodge. This enables it to be recorded in the minutes by the secretary and objected against if the members feel opposed to the proposition.

(c) In order to complete a record of the monies received and spent the Treasurer needs to maintain a record of the monies moving through all of the Lodge bank accounts. These should be kept up to date and take a format in which the treasurer is happy with. This may mean that you would like to write things up manually in a book or you might prefer to have them recorded electronically on a spreadsheet. Personally, I prefer an electronic format as the addition process can be simplified. However, you will need to ensure adequate backups are in place, and hard copies printed out for annual inspection by the lodge auditors. Also with electronic formats they can be stored in a remote electronic storage medium. Again to ensure a remote back up is in place, should there be any issues with the computer they are held on. There are various free options to do this so it becomes a cost free exercise.

(d) The preparation of the accounts can appear complex, but I hope that by taking the processes a step at a time it will help you to work through any issues you may have.

(e) Once you have prepared the lodge annual accounts you will need to have these audited by the appointed lodge auditors. This appointment is usually done by the Brethren at the same meeting in which the Master is installed. The Secretary will usually propose the appointment and once seconded it is the voted on. It is better that the more experienced Brethren of the Lodge carry out the audit, as many of the younger Brethren may not fully understand the procedures. The only time you may find that it would be more beneficial for the Lodge to have a junior member conduct the audit would be if he has the appropriate level of accounting expertise to justify his selection. This is going to be explained in more detail in Chapter 14.

(f) The accounts should be produced in a format that is consistent with previous years as implied by the term "mutatis mutandis". This means make only those changes that need to be changed. However, I would also say make sure that the format being used is clear and understandable. Therefore, if you believe the formats could be better understood by making subtle changes, then as the Treasurer you may make those changes. You also need to be aware that, as the Treasurer, you are responsible for any bank account that has the name of the Lodge in it; as such, each of these individual accounts needs to be included within the annual accounts presented to the Lodge. With most Lodge accounts, you will find you have several different pockets of monies, which will need to be accounted for separately. These are shown as different income and expenditure accounts as discussed later.

With the majority of new appointees to the office of Treasurer only having a basic understanding of accountancy, they will generally follow the formats and presentation laid down by the previous Treasurer. Therefore, it would not be hard to image that the current formats used by the Lodge may have most likely been used for many years and indeed by many different Treasurers. The formats may still be appropriate or not and you will need to decide. You are responsible for presenting the accounts annually to the Brethren. By making the accounts clear and self-explanatory, you may end up with fewer questions when they are presented to the Lodge. I have seen many versions of accounts with some looking familiar to my expectations and experience, but many in formats that I have not seen for years. This illustrates the habit of copying previous formats. Therefore, if you are still using horizontal income and expenditure account formats, you may wish to change them to the more commonly recognisable vertical format. The horizontal formats disappeared from use in public practice many years ago. The use of these formats is usually evident in some of the older lodges in the UK. The horizontal format is one, which has the receipts on the left hand side, and the payments on the right hand side, whereas the vertical format is one that shows the income on the top with the expenses below and deducted from the income to show either a surplus or a deficit.

To illustrate this I was recently at my Chapter meeting, when the Treasurer presented the accounts. I asked how he was going to address the deficits we had incurred for the last few years; he replied "what deficits?" The reason for his answer was that the format of the accounts showed the monies received and paid out as a summarised cashbook. At no point did it show whether there were any deficits or surpluses. Hence, we had been continually reducing our Chapter reserves without it being addressed. It was only when I reviewed the accounts and asked the question that the issue had been brought to light. Since then the subscriptions had to be increased by £5 for each member to prevent the erosion of Lodge funds. However small the increase it will never make you very popular!

The subscriptions are the main income for a Lodge to cover their costs. This means you need to collect all the subscriptions due for the year and make sure all costs are paid out without leaving the Lodge indebted. There should be no profit or loss, as a Lodge is ran for the benefit of its members. Therefore, the Lodge should aim to run as close to a breakeven point as possible, this means that all receipts are equal to the sums paid out. Setting the subscriptions at the start of a year will always have to be an estimation of the expected costs for the year and with this in mind you may end the year with either a small surplus or deficit.

If the surplus is too high, either there may be costs, which have not been paid out, or the subscriptions are too high for the costs you have incurred. It may be you have set the subscriptions higher for a specific reason, if this is the case no further amendment is required. If not, you may wish to consider reducing them. Conversely, if you are running at a deficit you will need to look at increasing the subscriptions to cover the shortfall. During the course of this book, I will go into more detail about calculating the breakeven figure, which will be discussed in chapter 13. The accounting terms like income and expenditure account, balance sheet and the need for main records to be kept will be explained in later chapters 6 – 7. The need for keeping general and charitable funds separate will be illustrated in chapter 8.

The key to being a Lodge Treasurer is to present accounts annually to the Lodge. This means summarising all movements in the year being presented. I will explain further how to do this in simple steps in chapter 12. It does not have to be complicated; far from it, the easier it is to follow, and the easier it will be for the Brethren to understand.

The need to have Lodge accounts examined by the audit committee is just a means of the Lodge members being assured that all is in order. Therefore, the examiners programme will give them a guide of what they should look for in the accounts (Chapter 14). The completion of tax returns can be daunting but again this is straight forward, and subject to agreement from the H M Revenue & Customs could be even easier. This is explained further, in chapter 15.

One final issue to consider is the requirements of the Data Protection Act 1998. The purpose of the act is to give guidelines to the uses and holders of data to ensure correct procedures are adhered to, all those who hold electronic data need to register, unless you qualify for one of the exemptions. As a non-profit making organisation and one, which only holds data for the processing of accounts and records, then a Lodge is protected by the exemption included in the guidelines on the Information Commissioners website (www.ico.gov.uk). If you are in any doubt, please refer directly to the website for further guidance. Finally, to make the earlier steps easier to follow, I have included examples of accounts layouts, cashbooks and other templates to make this a useful guide. The aim of this book is to give everyone a chance to become a Lodge Treasurer if they wish to, and give them the tools to help them to do it.

CHAPTER 2

GETTING STARTED
AND WHAT YOU NEED TO KNOW

The importance of this office first becomes apparent when you realise that the job of a Treasurer is one of only two offices within the Lodge that requires election annually by the members of the Lodge. The other one is that of the Worshipful Master.

Once elected under the Book of Constitutions Rule 112, what have you agreed to take on?

As Treasurer, the responsibilities that are expected of you are the following:

- Safe guarding the funds and assets of the lodge
- Ensuring all monies are banked promptly
- Collecting all the subscriptions due
- Paying all expenses incurred in due time
- Prepare budgets to help maintain solvency
- Production of annual accounts

The need for an understanding of double entry bookkeeping is not an essential requirement for the office of Treasurer. Double Entry Bookkeeping is considered to have been around since the 15th Century and remains mainly unchanged to this day, but you do not need to have a full understand of double entry bookkeeping to fulfil this office. Therefore it is my intention to help you in the role of lodge Treasurer without explaining the intricacies of debits and credits used in double entry bookkeeping. The majority of Lodges can operate on a simple receipts and payments summary. If you are the Treasurer of a Lodge that owns the building and have to operate VAT, you will probably require assistance from an accountant. For the non-accountants amongst you, this guide will help you through the records you need to keep as well as how to put together the annual accounts for presentation to the Lodge, and its members.

The first and most important thing to understand is the Lodge subscriptions. They should cover the core costs of Grand Lodge and Provincial or Metropolitan Lodge and the other costs for the year. The method of calculating this is further explained in chapter 13.

The core costs of most lodges will typically include:

- Hall rents
- Secretarial expenses

- Stewards/dining account
- Insurance
- Tyler costs (if applicable)
- Cost of Past Masters jewel
- Any replacement regalia
- Gratuities
- Miscellaneous other expenses

This list is not exhaustive, but covers the majority of the costs you would normally incur from the general account.

You may well have more than one bank account that you will be responsible for maintaining. They might include the following bank accounts:

Deposit account
- Stewards account
- Almoners/Charity/Benevolent account
- Ladies Festival account
- Grants account
- Charity Relief Chest account

Each of these accounts is set up for a particular reason, and used solely for that reason.

Deposit account
This would be set up to try to utilise any surplus monies you may have. At present, the possibility of a strong return on the monies held on deposit is minimal. In selecting, the correct type of account for any surplus monies held, the return required and security should always be a priority. If you are lucky enough to have an amount of cash that exceeds the limit of Financial Services Compensation Scheme (FSCS) then you might want to have this split between different banks. The FSCS is UK's compensation fund of last resort for customers of authorised financial services firms. (This includes monies held in bank deposit accounts) and preserves the bank balances in the event of any problems or collapse of any one particular bank. If, however, this necessitates the requirement of an additional account to be set up with a new bank, you will need to have this bank and branch approved by the members in open lodge by resolution.

The Steward's account
This would be set up to process and keep control of the finances relating to the festive board. This should always be kept with a positive balance, and used to prevent the costs getting out of control from the festive board.

Almoners/Charity/Benevolent account

This account is used to keep the funds separate from normal general funds. It serves two purposes. Firstly, to keep all charity monies separate from the normal funds and secondly, it will give the Almoner funds to help the causes that may wish to make a claim on the Lodge charity. The main purpose for keeping charity funds separate from the general account is that, if it is merged with general funds you may end up utilising charitable monies on non-charity or routine matters. If it is in a separate account, it clearly prevents this from happening.

Ladies Festival account

This is an optional account, which would give the ability to keep festival funds separate from the main account. It would also enable a festival secretary to maintain a record of all transactions for a specific event.

Grants account

This is another account used by the Almoner; it maintains privacy and confidentiality for any Lodge member and their relatives who receive monies from the four main Masonic Charities. This account should be clearly named 'Grants Account' to ensure the funds are kept separate from other charitable funds.

Charity Relief Chest account

The Charity Steward through the Grand Charity administers the Charity Relief Chest account. This is the account into which all of the regular monthly donations given by the brethren are deposited. However, as this account will bear the name of the Lodge it is the responsibility of the Treasurer to report on the movements in the annual accounts. The monies received in will be summarised, but will not be detailed to show who has given what. In fact, most of the movements are indeed summarised by the statement produced periodically by the Grand Charity. I have always used this summary for inclusion in the accounts.

From the accounts detailed above, I would anticipate you would need a minimum of a General account, an Almoners/Charity/Benevolent account, a Relief Chest account and a Grants account. You may well have additional accounts that can all be treated in their own way following the templates and guidelines in this book. As the Treasurer, you will need to record the movements on each of the accounts for each financial year. I will detail the requirements for each account in the next two chapters.

CHAPTER 3

RECORDS TO KEEP AND MAINTAIN

There is no need to use complex accounting software. In order to keep things simple, I would suggest that you could effectively use three documents to record the relevant transactions.

They are:

- Members register
- Cash book receipts
- Cash book payments

The members register covers many aspects of your responsibilities. I would suggest laying out the register as per Table 1.

The template gives an indication of the layout but you can tailor this to suit your own specific needs. Accurately maintaining the table ensures that you know who has paid their subscriptions and when. This way you can keep track of any outstanding fees. If you have members who wish to pay by direct debit to spread the cost and subject to the Lodge finances having enough spare funds to allow this, I would suggest showing the actual dates the payments are made. The above can be used in a hand written book, or if preferred a simple spreadsheet.

The total monies received from the members should also agree with the total shown from the bank receipts summary, which I will go through in the next chapter. By ensuring the totals agree you will know that you have not missed any members' subscriptions from the register.

One of the duties of a Treasurer is to make sure that all funds are recorded, so that should any member wishing to join another Lodge, the secretary is able to provide a clearance certificate as required. This certificate confirms that all dues are indeed paid, up to date. If a member has dues outstanding and another Lodge accepts that member into their Lodge, then the new Lodge becomes liable for the payment of those fees. This is noted in the Book of Constitutions Rule 163(d). Therefore the members register should also show the names of any member who has resigned or been excluded for non-payment of fees. That way if he requests to join another Lodge with any previous subscriptions still in arrears, he will not be granted the appropriate clearance certificates, unless payment is made to clear any outstanding subscriptions. I will go through in more detail in chapter

Table 1

Names of members	Contact details	Payment type	Date of joining	Brought Forward from previous year	Subs Due for this year	Joining fee	Amount paid	Date paid	Balance still due
Member 1	Such as	Monthly DDR	01/01/1970	20.00	120.00		120.00	12 x £10	20.00
Member 2	Telephone	Annual Cheque	01/01/1980	-	120.00		120.00	01/02/2010	-
Member 3	number	Cash	01/01/1990	-	120.00		120.00	01/03/2010	-
Member 4	email	Monthly DDR	01/01/2000	(20.00)	120.00		100.00	10 x £10	-
Member 5	or	Annual Cheque	01/01/2010	-	120.00	60.00	180.00	01/01/2010	-
Member 6	address etc	Resigned in Good standing on xx/xx/xx		-	-	-	-	00/01/2010	-
etc									
				-	600.00	60.00	640.00		20.00

11 what is required to exclude a member who has not paid his subscription for two years as explained in the Book of Constitutions Rule 148. The cashbook receipts and payments will be discussed in more detail in chapters 4 & 5.

As you can see the record keeping is straight forward, the members register is purely a record of all members, what is due, and what has been paid. You can expand the addresses or even use email addresses or telephone numbers as the primary contact point, if you wish. My Lodge accounts are made up to the 31st May each year, and our Lodge subscriptions become due on the 1st June each year. This means that the subscriptions become payable during the closed summer recess. Therefore, one trick I have found to help get the subscriptions in during the summer recess is to issue an invoice. This serves two purposes, the first being I am not chasing lots of subscriptions on the night of installation in October and secondly I do not get any excuses about them being unaware it was due. This is a simple and effective tool. It helps to save lots of time at the installation and gets the cheques in sooner.

An example of the wording and template I use is as follows:

Invoice for Lodge Subscription

Name & Address

Lodge subscriptions due for the year commencing 1st January 20XY

      Balance due   £XXX

Payment due on 1st January 20XY and this year's subscriptions is now due

---

As you can see, the invoice is not complicated and is a simple tool to make your life a little bit easier. Some Lodges include the dining fees in their annual subscription fees and this may give a larger annual subscription fee than those Lodges without dining fees. Given the rising costs of Freemasonry and especially the festive boards, it may be an option to offer the ability to have the Lodge subscriptions paid by a monthly standing order. This in itself should be easy enough for members to set up, especially with the advent of online banking facilities. All you will need to do is provide them with the amount payable each month and the bank account number and sort code. However, sometimes the lodge subscription will not divide easily by twelve. If this is the case, I suggest rounding it up to the nearest whole pound. Then any surplus for the year will just be carried forward. This is why keeping detailed records of when each receipt comes through is helpful. Spreading the cost makes it easier for any members who would be happier to have a small monthly payment rather than paying one big annual sum, as Lodges have many members in very different financial circumstances it enables more people to enjoy the Fraternity without the worry of large annual demands.

You may wish to have a template for them to complete and return, for you to send to the bank to action, in which case the below template may help.

SETTLEMENT OF SUBSCRIPTIONS BY STANDING ORDER

To (the name of your bank) .... Date of Payment: Monthly ....

Branch: xxxxxxxxxxxx

Code No.	Bank and Branch Title	Account to be Credited	Amount
xx-xx-xx	xxxxxxxx	XXXXX Lodge No. xxxx	£xxx.xx
	xxxxxxxx	Account No. xxxxxxxx	
	xxxxxxxx		

Please make the first
Payment on date .... and monthly thereafter

Debit to (name)Members details..................... Account Sort code...........................

Bank address .... Account number ....
....
.... Signature ....
Date ....

If your Lodge does have dining fees included within the subscriptions you may wish to keep a separate note of the costs incurred at the festive board against the monies collected, as this way you will have a record to support any increases to the Lodge subscriptions. Any subscription increase will never make you popular but you have to ensure the Lodge's finances are balanced. I will go through in more detail how to calculate a breakeven figure for Lodge subscriptions in a later chapter, as it is vital that you have the correct information to enable you to do the calculation. Hence, if you collect £100 per head per annum for dining and spend £110 per head per annum you will have an annual deficit of £10 per member to cover.

Any subscription increases will need to be discussed with the Lodge committee to see if they wish to increase the subscriptions to cover the deficit, or ensure the Steward is less generous in topping up the wine. Which in itself might make him less popular, but it will be a choice the Lodge committee will need to make. You can only put to them the information you have collated and make a suggestion. Any increase in Lodge subscriptions will usually be put to the members of the Lodge for approval, however, there may be a committee elected under Rule 154 to debate any increase. There may also be a restriction in your own Lodge by-laws to prevent you from deciding on imposing an increase without consultation. Once an increase is agreed upon, it is usual that a notice of motion be given at the meeting prior to the meeting in which your financial year ends. For example, if your Lodge meets monthly and your year-end is in December, you will need to give a notice of motion in November, and the vote will be conducted in December. That way you can increase the subscriptions from the 1st January. These months will have to be changed and altered depending on your own Lodge's circumstances. The details of how to prepare the cashbook receipts and payments will be explained in the next two chapters. These documents will effectively become the main records from which the annual accounts will be prepared.

CHAPTER 4

RECEIPTS AND INCOME

What is a receipt? This is any monies paid into the bank account and received by the Treasurer. Income is monies received which you then deduct expenses from; for example, Lodge subscriptions are collected so you can pay out general Lodge expenses. They are therefore income. In most cases, income and receipts will be the same thing, as all income is banked and treated as a receipt in the bank account. However, there may be some cases where the monies banked are not income. For example if monies are transferred between accounts this is a payment from one account and receipts into another, this is not income as it just represents movement of funds between accounts. The type of receipts you have received will depend on the type of bank accounts you are paying the monies into.

As mentioned in previous chapters you should normally have a minimum of three accounts to report on each year, these being:

- General account
- Charity/Almoners/Benevolent account
- Relief Chest account

The type of receipts you would normally have for each account are as follows:

- General account
  - ☐ Subscriptions
  - ☐ Initiation fees
  - ☐ Donation towards Lodge funds
  - ☐ Stewards account items
  - ☐ Interest on monies held in the bank account
  - ☐ Sundry items of income
  - ☐ Ladies festival ticket sales income

- Charity/Almoners/Benevolent account
  - ☐ Alms collected
  - ☐ Ladies festival donation
  - ☐ Charity donations

- ☐ Grants received
- ☐ Interest received on monies held
- ☐ Raffles monies collected for charity
- ☐ Other charitable monies

■ Relief Chest account
  - ☐ Interest received on monies held
  - ☐ Regular giving contributions
  - ☐ Gift Aid contributions

There may be additional account receipt headings to allocate items to, but the types shown above cover the majority of the classes of income you should expect to have within the accounts. The mechanism of recording these receipts for use in the preparation of the accounts is the next step. For this, we need to set up templates to record the day-to-day transactions, which will be summarised to form the basis of the income in the annual accounts. The format for recording the receipts is a table showing the date the transaction occurred and the description of what each transaction related to, this way there is evidence to confirm the allocation of the income into the various categories.

The following template is an example of how to layout the general account. As you can see, the format analyses the income between the various headings, the majority of the income being subscriptions from Lodge members. Table 2, opposite, is used to extract the income from the bank receipts, which follows through into the income and expenditure account in a later chapter.

The same format can be repeated for the charity account, which again is the basis for the income and expenditure account for the charity account. The main reason for keeping the charity monies separately from the general fund is so that monies donated for charitable causes do not end up getting used for Lodge expenses, or other non-charitable expenditure. It is also important when monies are donated for a specific purpose, the money is used for that purpose, and that purpose only, see Table 3 overleaf.

If there are any other accounts, they can be laid out in the same manner. I have also included the analysis of a Steward's and Ladies Festival account. As you can see, there are fewer columns for analysis as there are likely to be less income types for these funds. If you need more or less columns to analyse the receipts you can amend as necessary, as shown in Table 4 overleaf.

Table 2

My Lodge Accounts number XXXX

Main fund receipts for the year 31st December 20XY

Date			Total	Subs 20XY	Subs 20XX	Initiation fees	Donation	Monies for lodge funds	Stewards account	Transfers from savings account	Interest	Sundries
01/01/XY	Member 1	Direct debit	120.00	120.00								
01/01/XY	Member 2	Direct debit	120.00	120.00								
01/01/XY	Member 3	Direct debit	120.00	120.00								
01/01/XY	Member 4	Direct debit	120.00	120.00								
01/01/XY	etc etc	Direct debit	1,200.00	1,200.00								
15/01/XY	Member 15	Cash	120.00	120.00								
15/01/XY	Member 16	Cash	120.00	120.00								
31/01/XY	Member 17	Cheque	240.00	120.00	120.00							
31/01/XY	Member 18	Cheque	120.00	120.00								
31/01/XY	Transfer from savings account	Transfer	1,000.00							1,000.00		
01/02/XY	Member 5	Direct debit	120.00	120.00								
02/02/XY	Member 19	Cheque	120.00	120.00								
05/02/XY	Member 20	Cheque	120.00	120.00								
28/02/XY	Surplus from Stewards account		1.53						1.53			
28/02/XY	Member 24	Cheque	200.00	120.00		80.00						
01/03/XY	Member 6	Direct debit	120.00	120.00								
11/03/XY	Member 7	Direct debit	120.00	120.00								
30/06/XY	Bank interest received		25.47								25.47	
31/08/XY	Summer BBQ money		159.64					159.64				
30/09/XY	Donation to lodge funds		125.00				125.00					
31/12/XY	Other receipt		1.23									1.23
			4,392.87	2,880.00	120.00	80.00	125.00	159.64	1.53	1,000.00	25.47	1.23

Table 3

My Lodge Accounts number XXXX

Charity/Almoners/Benevolent receipts for the year ended 31st December 20XY

Date		Total	Alms collected	Donations	Ladies festival	Interest received	Masonic Grants Received	Raffles received
31/01/XY	Alms Collected	25.23	25.23					
31/01/XY	Lodge Raffle	155.00						155.00
28/02/XY	Alms Collected	28.36	28.36					
28/02/XY	Lodge Raffle	125.00						125.00
31/03/XY	Alms Collected	33.11	33.11					
31/03/XY	Lodge Raffle	165.00						165.00
30/04/XY	Alms Collected	18.12	18.12					
30/04/XY	Lodge Raffle	95.00						95.00
15/04/XY	Raffle from ladies night	1,250.00			1,250.00			
30/06/XY	Summer Grants	150.00					150.00	
30/06/XY	Bank interest - Gross of tax	12.21				12.21		
30/09/XY	Alms Collected	20.01	20.01					
30/09/XY	Lodge Raffle	110.00						110.00
31/10/XY	Alms Collected	55.15	55.15					
31/10/XY	Lodge Raffle	200.00						200.00
30/11/XY	Alms Collected	36.89	36.89					
30/11/XY	Lodge Raffle	145.00						145.00
31/12/XY	Alms Collected	42.85	42.85					
31/12/XY	Lodge Raffle	170.00						170.00
31/12/XY	Winter Grants	150.00					150.00	
31/12/XY	Donation to widows gifts	50.00		50.00				
		3,036.93	259.72	50.00	1,250.00	12.21	300.00	1,165.00

Table 4

My Lodge Accounts number XXXX

Steward Account & Ladies festival receipts for the year ended 31st December 20XY

Date	Details	Total	Interest received	Ticket sales	Stewards funds collected	Other income
31/01/XY	Festive Board monies	360.00			360.00	
28/02/XY	Festive Board monies	390.00			390.00	
31/03/XY	Festive Board monies	420.00			420.00	
30/04/XY	Festive Board monies	375.00			375.00	
15/04/XY	Raffle from ladies night	5,250.00		5,250.00		
15/04/XY	Tombola / raffle monies	-				
30/06/XY	Bank interest - Gross of tax	0.01	0.01			
30/09/XY	Festive Board monies	490.00			490.00	
31/10/XY	Festive Board monies	345.00			345.00	
30/11/XY	Festive Board monies	330.00			330.00	
31/12/XY	Festive Board monies	315.00			315.00	
		-				
		8,275.01	0.01	5,250.00	3,025.00	-

CHAPTER 5

PAYMENTS AND EXPENSES

Payments are easier to define. They are monies paid out on behalf of the Lodge. The main thing you need to remember with payments is that you will need to ensure they are allocated to the correct the type of payment. As in the previous chapter regarding receipts, the same principles follow with the payments. The latest revision to the rule 153 in the Book of Constitution now requires all cheque payments have two signatories, one of which must be the treasurer unless impractical. This means that all cheques have to be countersigned and verified that they are for the purposes that they were intended. Your own Lodge by-laws may allow one signature on each cheque. It would be better for the Lodge to follow the Rule 153 and adopt the policy of having two signatories. This works as a control on behalf of the Lodge. If you are changing the lodge by-laws, you may want to adopt the use of electronic payments. This is now part of the new revised rule 153. There is however a strict requirement to have payments made electronically. This requires approval of the Lodge members in open Lodge as previously mentioned.

As before, most items paid out of an account are expenses, which are then deducted from the income received, but there will be transfers between accounts, which are just a movement of funds and hence not an expense. The authority for paying out normal expenditure falls with the Treasurer only. The Treasurer, up to an agreed nominal sum, can usually pay out some non-normal expenditure. This should be defined within the by-laws of the lodge. However, this may need to be reviewed, as it may not have been updated for many years.

You may find that you only have authority for such a small nominal sum in today's terms that it would render the by-laws almost worthless. If this is the case, you will need to ask the Secretary to go through the appropriate procedures to increase the authority limit. If the payments are more substantial and not part of the normal expenditure, these payments will require the relevant notice of motion at one meeting and the voting on at the following meeting after it has been proposed and seconded.

The most common types of payments from the three main accounts as noted in the previous chapter are as follows:

- ■ General account
  - ☐ Grand Lodge dues
  - ☐ Provincial or Metropolitan Lodge dues
  - ☐ Lodge rent
  - ☐ Secretarial expenses
  - ☐ Ritual books
  - ☐ Book of Constitutions
  - ☐ Regalia
  - ☐ Past Master's jewels
  - ☐ Insurance
  - ☐ Gifts and gratuities
  - ☐ Tyler's cost
  - ☐ Sundry other items

- ■ Charity / Almoners / Benevolent account
  - ☐ Almoners costs
  - ☐ Widows gifts
  - ☐ Payments to Masonic charities
  - ☐ Payments to other charities

- ■ Relief Chest account
  - ☐ Payments to Masonic charities
  - ☐ Payments to other charitable causes

As you can see, there are more payment types for the general fund, as these tend to cover the costs incurred in running the Lodge. These items you hope to control as the Treasurer, to prevent the ever-increasing cost of Lodge subscriptions, or suffer the continual erosion of Lodge funds. As in the previous chapter, the formats are the same, but I have included these as examples to follow showing the analysis of the expenses in the different type of bank accounts. The headings cover the primary headings as listed above but if you need any additional headings then you can amend the column headings as necessary. You will also note that the total is in one column, with the expense allocated to its respective column. The reason for this is that you will then have the total for inclusion income and expenditure account, which will be put together in the next chapter from the examples in Tables 5, 6 and 7

Table 5

My Lodge Accounts number XXXX
Main fund payments for the year 31st December 20XY

Date		Cheque number	Total	Grand Lodge dues	Provincial Grand Lodge	Lodge rent	Secretarial expenses	Regalia & Ritual expenses	Christmas gifts	Other Gifts	Insurance	Sundries	Tyler
31/01/XY	Tyler fees	102136	10.00										10.00
31/01/XY	Provincial Lodge fees	102137	224.00		224.00								
28/02/XY	Tyler fees	102138	10.00										10.00
28/02/XY	Raffle tickets	102139	5.98									5.98	
31/03/XY	Tyler fees	102140	10.00										10.00
31/03/XY	Book of Constitution	102141	10.00					10.00					
30/04/XY	Tyler fees	102142	10.00										10.00
31/05/XY	Regalia Insurance	102143	70.00								70.00		
30/06/XY	Gift for tyler	102144	15.00							15.00			
31/08/XY	Grand Lodge fees	102145	952.00	952.00									
30/09/XY	Tyler fees	102146	10.00										10.00
31/10/XY	Tyler fees	102147	10.00										10.00
30/11/XY	Tyler fees	102148	10.00										10.00
30/11/XY	Secretarial expenses	102149	32.22				32.22						
30/11/XY	Christmas donation	102150	25.00						25.00				
31/12/XY	Tyler fees	102151	10.00										10.00
31/12/XY	Lodge rents	102152	1,820.00			1,820.00							
			3,234.20	952.00	224.00	1,820.00	32.22	10.00	25.00	15.00	70.00	5.98	80.00

Table 6

My Lodge Accounts number XXXX

Almoners/Charity/ Benevolent fund payments for the year ended 31st December 20XY

Date		chq number	Total	Almoner expenses & Flowers	Masonic Charities	Master's charity	Masonic Grants paid out	Sundries
30/06/XY	National Smartians Funds	100215	250.00		250.00			
30/06/XY	Summer Grant payment	100216	150.00				150.00	
30/09/XY	Flowers for Mrs Heinz	100217	10.00	10.00				
30/11/XY	Provincial Grand Charity	100218	500.00		500.00			
31/05/XY	Flowers for Mrs Hovis	100219	15.00	15.00				
31/12/XY	Macmillian Cancer relief	100220	750.00			750.00		
31/12/XY	Breast Cancer research	100221	1,000.00			1,000.00		
31/12/XY	Winter Grant payment	100222	150.00				150.00	
			2,825.00	25.00	750.00	1,750.00	300.00	-

Table 7

My Lodge Accounts number XXXX

Stewards account and Ladies festival payments for the year ended 31st December 20XY

Date		chq number	Total	Entertainment costs	Ladies gifts	Flowers	Transfers	Ladies night meal	Festive board costs	Sundries
31/01/XY	Festive Board monies	100208	359.22						359.22	
28/02/XY	Festive Board monies	100209	389.25						389.25	
28/02/XY	Surplus transferred to general account	100210	1.53				1.53			
31/03/XY	Festive Board monies	100211	419.19						419.19	
30/04/XY	Festive Board monies	100212	374.22						374.22	
15/04/XY	Disco costs	100213	300.00	300.00						
15/04/XY	Ladies night gifts	100214	222.50		222.50					
15/04/XY	Ladies night meals	100215	4,497.50					4,497.50		
15/04/XY	Raffle tickets	100216	4.99							4.99
15/04/XY	Ladies night flowers	100217	225.00			225.00				
30/09/XY	Festive Board monies	100218	492.15						492.15	
31/10/XY	Festive Board monies	100219	342.22						342.22	
30/11/XY	Festive Board monies	100220	328.84						328.84	
31/12/XY	Festive Board monies	100221	316.11						316.11	
			8,272.72	300.00	222.50	225.00	1.53	4,497.50	3,021.20	4.99

CHAPTER 6

INCOME AND EXPENDITURE ACCOUNT

The term income and expenditure account sounds familiar, in the sense we have all heard it before, but at the same time you would not necessarily know how to go about preparing one. It is just a summary of the income monies received and the expense payments made during a certain period. Especially if you are just recording the income received and expenses paid out on a purely cash received and paid basis. This means you can easily extract the income from the cashbook receipts summary and the expenses from the cashbook payment summary. Typically, the income is analysed using the headings on the receipts in the cashbook. It is for this reason you have as many columns in the cashbooks as the types of income you have. The number of columns is not a restricting factor on a spreadsheet, but if you use a book, its width and the number of columns in it will limit the size restriction of an actual book. If, you find you need more columns than in the book you can simply divide them up in the various columns to give the additional detail you want in the income and expenditure account. The same is then applied to the payments, albeit you may have more groups of expenditure you wish to include and therefore they can be sub-divided into more detail for the income and expenditure account as required. Having given the examples of the cash receipts and payments in the previous two chapters, I will now use these to give examples of how the income and expenditure accounts are collated from the cashbooks.

I will start with the General account, which was the first summary of receipts in chapter 4. I started by saying that all receipts are not income. Income is the monies used to pay the expenses. I have illustrated this with the total amount of receipts in the general account cashbook. The total shown in chapter 4 for the receipts was £4,392.87, but as you will see from the income and expenditure account, the total income is only £3,392.87. The difference between the two was the £1,000, which was transferred in from the deposit account. Therefore when preparing the income and expenditure account you will use the income figure received of £3,392.87 and not the monies banked of £4,392.87, as shown in Table 8 overleaf. The movement in the monies between bank accounts can also be seen when we look at the balance sheet in chapter 7.

Table 8

My Lodge Accounts number XXXX				
Summary of Receipts and Payments for the **General Fund for the year ended 31st December 20XY**				
	20XY		20XX	
	£	£	£	£
Receipts				
Subscriptions		3,000.00		2,760.00
Initiation fees		80.00		80.00
Interest		25.47		22.33
Summer BBQ		159.64		185.34
Stewards account		1.53		2.33
Other receipts		-		12.00
Sundry receipts		1.23		2.22
Donation		125.00		125.00
		3,392.87		3,189.22
Payments				
Grand Lodge	952.00		952.00	
Prov. or Met. Grand Lodge	224.00		224.00	
Lodge rents	1,820.00		1,820.00	
Secretary's Expenses	32.22		35.32	
Regalia & Ritual	10.00		10.00	
Christmas/Gratuities	25.00		25.00	
Gifts & Appeals	15.00		15.00	
Insurance	70.00		70.00	
Sundries	5.98		2.99	
Tyler	80.00		80.00	
		(3,234.20)		(3,234.31)
Excess / (deficit) for the year		158.67		(45.09)

As you can see, the expenses represent the total payments on the cashbook.

The Almoners/Charity/Benevolent account is a little simpler. You will see that the total of the income represents all the monies banked from chapter 4 and likewise the payments represent all the monies paid out from chapter 5 in the respective columns as shown in Table 9 opposite.

The next account to analyse is the Steward's and Ladies festival account. As you can see the total of the receipts and payments in this bank account agree with the totals from the earlier chapters. The only point I would make, is that any surplus or deficit would need to be transferred to or from the general account. I have illustrated this with a small surplus being paid out as an expense in this bank account, which is shown as income in the General fund account. You might note that the figure for transfer between this account and the general account does not

Table 9

My Lodge Accounts number XXXX				
Summary of Receipts and Payments for the Almoners/Charity/ Benevolent Account Fund for the year ended 31st December 20XY				
	20XY		**20XX**	
	£	£	£	£
Receipts				
Alms Collections		259.72		240.33
Donations		50.00		50.00
Ladies Festival Raffle		1,250.00		1,000.00
Interest		12.21		9.53
Masonic Grants		300.00		300.00
Lodge raffle		1,165.00		1,050.00
		3,036.93		2,649.86
Payments				
Almoner costs and Flo	25.00		35.00	
Masonic Charities	750.00		500.00	
Master's Charity	1,750.00		1,750.00	
Provincial Grants	300.00		300.00	
Sundries	-		-	
		(2,825.00)		(2,585.00)
Excess / (deficit) for the year		211.93		64.86

equal the surplus from the income and expenditure from the previous year. The reason being is you may wish to retain a surplus within the account for future events. The sum is used only as a guide to provide details of where the entries should appear if you had to transfer a surplus. It maybe that you do not wish to leave any surplus in this account, in which case the net income and expenditure account will be zero as the surplus or deficit is taken to or from the general account as required. See Table 10 overleaf.

As mentioned in a previous chapter, the Relief Chest account summary is provided by the Grand Charity. You can then use this summary to prepare a summary for inclusion within the accounts for the lodge. However, in order to give the final worked example, I have also drawn up one to illustrate the format and layout for you, Table 11 overleaf.

Table 10

My Lodge Accounts number XXXX

Summary of Receipts and Payments for the
Steward And Ladies Festival Fund for the year ended 31st December 20XY

	20XY		20XX	
	£	£	£	£
Receipts				
Ticket sales		5,250.00		5,400.00
Interest received		0.01		0.01
Festive Board Monies received		3,025.00		3,300.00
Donation		-		50.00
		8,275.01		8,750.01
Payments				
Ladies night meal costs	4,497.50		4,672.37	
Festive board costs	3,021.20		3,305.30	
Entertainment costs	300.00		300.00	
Ladies gifts	222.50		225.00	
Flowers	225.00		200.00	
Transfer surplus	1.53		2.33	
Sundries	4.99		-	
		(8,272.72)		(8,705.00)
Excess / (deficit) for the year		2.29		45.01

Table 11

My Lodge Accounts number XXXX

Summary of Receipts and Payments for the
Relief Chest Fund for the year ended 31st December 20XY

	20XY		20XX	
	£	£	£	£
Receipts				
Donations received		1,500.00		1,600.00
Interest received		122.50		113.03
Gift aid contribution		375.00		400.00
		1,997.50		2,113.03
Payments				
Monies paid to Grand Charity	1,500.00		500.00	
Monies paid to Provincial Grand Charity	-		1,000.00	
		(1,500.00)		(1,500.00)
Excess / (deficit) for the year		497.50		613.03

CHAPTER 7

BALANCE SHEET

What is a Balance Sheet? It is a well-known phrase but not many people understand how these are put together. I once visited a Lodge where the annual accounts were being presented to the Brethren, and when I looked at them the total of the column of figures on the top did not equal the total of the figures on the bottom, which they should do. As I knew the Treasurer I went up afterwards and quietly asked him, why they did not balance and his response to this was "should they?" To which I responded, "Yes!" The balance sheet is a record of the assets, liabilities and retained funds at a point in time. In this case, the financial year end of the Lodge. Now historically the balance sheet was horizontal with all the Debits on the left and the Credits on the right. This is a very unfamiliar method of producing accounts now. The current preference is to have assets less liabilities on the top half and retained funds on the bottom.

The main headings of a balance sheet are Fixed Assets and Investments, Current Assets, Current Liabilities and the Retained Funds. A typical format would be as per Table 12 below:

	£	£
Fixed Assets	1,000.00	
Investments	4,125.00	
		5,125.00
Current assets		
Outstanding dues	250.00	
Bank accounts	11,250.00	
Cash	50.00	
		11,550.00
Current liabilities		
Secretary expenses		(125.00)
		16,550.00
Represented by:-		
Retained Funds		
General Fund		4,350.00
Almoner's Fund		1,500.00
Steward's Account		150.00
Relief chest		10,550.00
		16,550.00

Table 12

As you will see, the top subtotal figure adds up to the same number as the bottom subtotal figure. Now in most cases you should only have one bank account for each fund. That way the net movement on the bank account will equal the movement in the income and expenditure account. For example, you may start with no money in a bank account and no other assets or liabilities, and receive all the subscriptions in one night of, say, £2,000. This is a dream for all Treasurers. You have a net income with no expenses of £2,000 and £2,000 in the bank account.

Therefore, your General account shows the information in Table 13.

Table 13

Subscriptions	£2,000
Net income for the period	£2,000
The Balance Sheet then shows	
Bank Account	£2,000
Retained funds	
- General Fund (from above)	2,000

As you can see, the two halves of the balance sheet agree. This is effectively how it works. If you now show a total amount of payments to be made which totals £1,700, you would only be left with £300 in the bank account and this would give you a surplus of £300 for the year. Therefore, it would then look as Table 14.

Table 14

Subscriptions	£2,000
Various expenses	(£1,700)
Net income for the period	£300
The Balance Sheet then shows	
Bank Account	£300
Retained funds	
- General Fund (from above)	£300

Then each year thereafter, the net surplus / deficit would add to or deduct from the bank account and retained funds from the previous year. This way all the funds are built up.

The types of headings shown in the first example need a little more explanation.

- Fixed assets are items of Lodge furniture or other items which you have invested in and expect to be used for many years to come.
- Investments would be long-term items, such as shares, unit trusts or property. These are for the purpose of generating growth in capital value and developing some additional investment income.
- Current assets are the unpaid dues from Lodge members or debtors, monies in the bank accounts and cash held. The only other item you might want to include is stock of any books, but this is a little excessive for simple accounts.
- Current liabilities are monies you owe or creditors. This might be dining fees, Secretary's fees etc. In most cases you will pay expenses as they are due so you are unlikely to have any current liabilities if the accounts are prepared on a simple receipts and payments basis, but if you did have any this is where they belong.
- Retained funds are the balancing items on the balance sheet. To expand this further the net movement between the total assets less liabilities from one year to the next would be equal to the surplus or deficit for the current year. This means that the retained fund becomes the balancing item on the balance sheet to show that all the entries have been reflected in both the balance sheet and the income and expenditure account. This ensures completeness in the entries and that all debits and credits have been included in the respective headings.

As you can, see most of the items can be grouped into the selective areas. You may wish to separate them for a clearer understanding, or may wish to amalgamate all the bank accounts into one figure for the presentation of the accounts. The only disadvantage with this is that you may well end up with people saying, "If you have all that money in the accounts why don't you reduce the subscriptions?" In fact, most of the money held is on behalf of the charitable causes and therefore not free funds available for the running of the Lodge.

If you take on the role of Treasurer and are not an accountant, then I would always operate on a cash basis for preparing accounts, so you would only record the movement on the bank accounts. This way you will never have to worry about balancing the balance sheet with any unpaid dues/subscriptions. The net movement in the bank account will be the net movement in the various funds shown at the bottom of the balance sheet.

There is another method of accounting for transactions; this is referred to as the accrual concept. This method is a more complex way of accounting for simple accounts, and it would probably necessitate the use of an extended trial balance. There is an example of the layout at the back of the book. However, I would suggest it is better left to the accountants or those with accounting experience.

You may ask, "Why use a balance sheet?" Well, the purpose of a balance sheet is a check to ensure all items have been accounted for and that all items have been analysed within the income and expenditure account. One of the ways to trace the difference is to do a bank reconciliation, which I intend to go through in chapter 9. As illustrated above, the balance sheet just reflects the monetary movements from the income and expenditure account for each year. When it does not balance with the movement on the income and expenditure account it maybe that you have not recorded something in either the cash receipts or payments (which would show as extra money in the bank accounts or other assets). For example, in chapter four, we went through the analysis of the monies received into the general fund current account. Now in this example the total receipts was £4,392.87, but the figure for the income and expenditure account we only had a total income of £3,392.87. The difference being exactly £1,000.00. The reason for this is that it represented the transfer of monies from a savings account to a general account. This can be seen in the working example below of the balance sheet. Using the previous year's figures, we have two bank accounts under the heading of general fund. In the current year, we only have one account balance, but the increase from the previous year's figure is the surplus from the income and expenditure account of £158.67 and £1,000.00 transferred from the deposit account. (£1,220.13 + £158.67 + 1,000.00 = £2,378.80). I hope this is all understandable and can be followed easily. In essence, you now have the logic to follow and complete a balance sheet from the previous year's figures is shown in Table 15.

The only problem you may have with completing the first balance sheet is that you do not know where to start from, especially if your predecessor has not completed one. What I would suggest is that you start by looking at the balance on the bank accounts at the end of the previous year. Make a note of the different fund types in the different accounts and this will give you the top half of the balance sheet on a purely cash accounting basis. The item you will not know is the retained funds brought forward for each fund type. However, if the accounts are prepared on the cash basis, then the balance on the retained funds is the balance on the bank account. The reason you have a balance on the bank accounts is the accumulation of the excess of the surpluses and deficits of money over a number of years. This is then just the balancing figure. You now have a balanced balance sheet to start from.

Table 15

My Lodge Accounts number XXXX				
Balance sheet				
As at 31st December 31st December 20XY				
		20XY		20XX
Current Assets	£	£	£	£
General Fund				
Bank Accounts		2,378.80		1,220.13
Deposit account		-		1,000.00
Almoners Account		1,235.12		1,023.19
Ladies Festival & Stewards Account		558.31		556.02
Relief Chest Account		7,960.74		7,463.24
Total Assets		12,132.97		11,262.58
Represented by:-				
General fund				
Balance Brought Forward	2,220.13		2,265.22	
Excess / (deficit) for the year	158.67		(45.09)	
		2,378.80		2,220.13
Almoners/Charity/Benevolent Fund				
Balance Brought Forward	1,023.19		958.33	
Excess / (deficit) for the year	211.93		64.86	
		1,235.12		1,023.19
Ladies festival and stewards fund				
Balance Brought Forward	556.02		511.01	
Excess / (deficit) for the year	2.29		45.01	
		558.31		556.02
Relief Chest				
Balance Brought Forward	7,463.24		6,850.21	
Excess / (deficit) for the year	497.50		613.03	
		7,960.74		7,463.24
		12,132.97		11,262.58

CHAPTER 8

THE NEED TO KEEP
CHARITY FUNDS SEPARATE

One of the key principles of Freemasonry is Charity. As you have often heard, it said all the principles of Freemasonry are "Brotherly Love, Relief & Truth". The Relief aspect is the monies we give to Charity. During any year, you will have many pounds collected for charity and these will be for different causes. Therefore, one of the objectives is to keep all the funds separate from the general fund and to ensure that the monies collected are donated to the causes they were given for. This is why the best action is to keep all Charity monies in a separate bank account away from general funds. You will also need to record the details of whom the monies are collected for at each event. The monies, which brethren give through the regular payment promise, which the Charity Steward administers, all goes through the Relief Chest account, which is administered by the Grand Charity. In order to qualify for the reclaim of the tax through the gift aid system, donations have to be donated to a Charity registered with the Charities Commission.

Gift Aid is an incentive from the UK government enabling the monies paid over from taxed income to be grossed up. For example, as the basic rate of tax is currently 20% this means that the balance left after tax is 80%. Therefore, if donations are made and they qualify for Gift Aid, the monies donated are increased by 25%. This means when a donation of £5 is given and qualifies for gift aid the Inland Revenue will pay back to the Charity £1.25 as long as the donor states he is a basic rate tax payer. This is worked out by taking the 20%/80% ratio, which gives the 25%, which is received from the Inland Revenue. If the basic rate of tax changes, then so will the percentage received from the Inland Revenue. However, in order to qualify for gift aid payments you need to be a Registered Charity, therefore most individual Lodges will not be a Registered Charity in their own right, but will be affiliated with the main Charity within their province or district. In order to capitalise on this you may wish to have a collection on behalf of the cause of a charity at the end of a meeting, but if you obtain the appropriate Gift Aid envelopes from your own Provincial or District Charity and make the payments to them, they can then complete the appropriate forms and submit this to the HMRC. Once in receipt of this, the Gift Aid monies will be paid over to the Provincial or District Charity and then the respective charity could make the payment out on your behalf and supplement the monies donated.

The advantage in doing this is that any monies donated to a charity with the gift aid scheme can claim an uplift in the monies received of 25%. With the staggering sums donated by Freemasons each year, this helps to lift the figure even higher. There is also an additional benefit to any higher or additional rate taxpayers in that they will see the effective cost of the donation decrease, as they will be able to claim additional tax relief on the donations on their own personal income tax return. If you consider the cycle of festivals that the various Provinces or Districts support, by donating through the Relief Chest scheme a Province or District can lift its giving from, say, £2m to £2.5m, an increase of 25%. This would necessitate all donations being made under the gift aid scheme, which is probably unlikely to be the case with all of the monies donated, but you can understand the level of increase that can be achieved by utilising the Gift Aid Scheme.

During the course of a year you may have monies raised for different causes, being either Masonic or Non-Masonic charities. It is important that all the monies raised are correctly recorded, as when they need to be allocated; you should know how much was received for which charity. When any charity raffle is undertaken, the Brethren should always be made aware of the charity the money is being collected for, as the cause may stir certain emotions so people feel they would really wish to donate to, or in some cases, they may feel so strongly against it that they may not wish to donate. Whatever the case may be, you need to keep a separate record of the monies received and held in a separate charity bank account. You may even wish to show the separate charity monies held for later distribution, but I would suggest that this be kept as a memorandum account showing the breakdown of the fund. This is more often seen in charity accounts when monies are donated and given to a specific charity for a specific cause. The Charities Act 2011 stipulates that it can only be used for that purpose. You will often see terms like "designated" or "restricted" applied to Charity accounts. This is just simply the mechanism of allocating the separate pots of money to separate items of income or expenditure. This is then scaled down to the lodge charity accounts. Restricted funds are those monies given and assigned to a specific purpose by the donor, that is to say it can only be used for the purpose, which they were donated. On the other hand, a designated fund is earmarked for a particular purpose. Other than that, all funds are just general funds.

The best way to illustrate the different funds is at the end of a meeting, or at the festive board, where it is common to collect Alms. Alms are considered the monies donated for a general purpose to help those less fortunate that ourselves. In this sense, this would be best described as a general fund. If you had a raffle in favour of collecting monies to buy a gift for the Lodge Widows at Christmas, there would be no restriction on what the gift would be, but the monies must be allocated to the Lodge Widows. In this case, you would describe this as a designated fund, which is earmarked for a particular purpose, but there is no restriction on whether it is a gift voucher, chocolates or a bottle of wine. Finally, if you had a raffle for a particular cause, say a specific charity such as Macmillan Cancer relief, Help for Heroes, Breast Cancer, Prostate Cancer etc., then the monies collected would have to be paid for that specific purpose. Hence, this is a restricted donation to be applied only for the purpose it is donated. It is for this reason the purpose of the raffle should always be mentioned prior to the sale of any raffle tickets.

Therefore, during the course of a year there could be six raffles at the Festive Board, a Ladies night function in which there was a tombola and an auction for the Master's designated charity as indicated in Table 16 below.

Table 16

You might have collected the following amounts:-

Date	Amount
01.01.XY	155.00
01.02.XY	165.00
01.03.XY	135.00
01.04.XY	450.00
01.10.XY	180.00
01.11.XY	205.00
01.12.XY	190.00
	1,480.00

However without recording what they were for, the wrong amount may go to the wrong cause.

Therefore it would be better to record it as follows:-

Date		Amount
01.01.XY	Provincial Charity	155.00
01.02.XY	Charity A	165.00
01.03.XY	Charity B	135.00
01.04.XY	Charity B	450.00
01.10.XY	Charity A	180.00
01.11.XY	Charity B	205.00
01.12.XY	Charity B	190.00
		1,480.00

From this, you will know that the Provincial Charity will receive £155.00, Charity A will get £345.00 and Charity B receives £980.00, totalling the £1,480.00 collected over the various events. As you can see in the above example these are all monies donated for a restricted purpose. The purposes or charities are all different, but cheques need to be paid out for that purpose and that purpose only. In a normal set of registered charity accounts you would see these as separate funds with the monies paid in and out against them, but as we are not completing formal charity accounts we can amalgamate the monies paid in and out in the same Charity/Almoners/Benevolent income and expenditure account. You will however have to maintain the correct payments and match these to the income received. You may however have the appropriate by-law in place allowing you to top up the £980.00 above to a round £1,000.00; this will mean you will have authority to take the balance needed from the general funds donated. If you do not have the appropriate authority to do so, you will then have to apply to the Lodge at a regular meeting and have it voted on. Once the required notice of motion has been given in open Lodge, proposed and seconded you can then top up the monies drawn upon. As you can see particular care and attention needs to be taken with charity monies. You as the Treasurer are responsible for their safekeeping and to ensure they are given for the purpose they were intended for and applied only to the correct charitable purposes. I hope this helps to explain why charitable funds always need to be kept separate from general funds.

If you find that your lodge has always amalgamated the monies into one account you should take steps to separate the previous monies donated into a new bank account. Obviously, you will have to go through the required notice of motion in open Lodge to agree a new bank account at a branch convenient to yourself. Once notice has been given and the vote approved in open Lodge, you can then open the account and move the monies over. It is at this point you may well encounter a problem, as unless you have a separate record of what has been donated for what purpose and what has been paid out on the specific or general purpose previously, you are going to struggle to identify the correct balance to transfer over to the new charity/benevolent bank account. I cannot offer any specific guidance on this particular matter. All that can be done is to go through the previous accounts and work out the balance. The problem comes when you have an old Lodge with no records available prior to a certain point in time, then you are technically stuck.

However, as a practical solution to what I hope is a very rare problem, I would suggest you work out a rough approximation, put a schedule together and circulate this to the brethren. Give a notice of motion explaining what you intend to do and vote on the notice of motion at the next regular meeting, and transfer the best approximation you have. This is not an ideal situation, but it will enable a line to be drawn and to maintain the correct records going forward. I hope this helps to illustrate the need for accurate record keeping. It may be laborious, but in this instance, it will prove to be invaluable.

CHAPTER 9

ACCOUNTING PROCEDURES TO FOLLOW

With simple receipts and payments accounting, the main aspect with cashbooks is the need for the control accounts to work and the bank account to reconcile. This sounds complex but is just a set of procedures, which are laid down to ensure the completeness of entries.

In chapter 4 and 5, we went through the various summaries of the receipts and payments for each bank account. I showed how the total amount was allocated between the different headings in the accounts for both receipts and payments. What was probably not obvious in chapter 7 was how these movements are reflected in the bank balances in the balance sheet. To illustrate this we have a control account for each bank account. Therefore, I will show you the worked example for each bank account. It will help to demonstrate where the entries come from.

A control account has to start with an opening balance. To this, we then add the total monies received for the year and take away the total payments. This then gives a total at the bottom or the balance carried forward to the following year. I have illustrated this in Table 17 below.

Bank control account	
Opening balance	150.00
Total receipts	1,200.00
Total payments	(1,150.00)
Closing balance	200.00

Table 17

This is a simple control account but effectively summarises the entries made.

Now if we apply the same logic to the General fund example we can see how the movements in the total receipts and payments appear in the control account, Table 18.

Table 18

General lodge account	Current	Deposit
	£	£
Opening balance	1,220.13	1,000.00
Total receipts	4,392.87	-
Total payments	(3,234.20)	(1,000.00)
Closing balance	2,378.80	-

You can see from the above figures that the opening balance represents the figures in the balance sheet for the previous year. Therefore, the starting figure for one year is the closing balance from the previous year. This way you ensure continuity and no omissions. The total receipts and payments are the totals from the extracts included in chapters 4 and 5. You then have a closing balance at the end of the accounting year, which forms part of the bank accounts at the balance sheet date. The other point to note is that the total receipts are £1,000.00 less than the total income shown in the income and expenditure account in chapter 6. This is again because the summary of receipts in chapter 4 included a transfer in from a deposit account. I have therefore reflected this in the control account movement on the deposit account; i.e. the total payments shows the monies transferred into the current account.

Now, the purpose of the control account is to ensure all entries that have passed through the bank account for the year have been recorded correctly. In order to make sure that the control account is carrying out its function we need to agree it to the respective bank accounts. This is called the bank reconciliation, and again it sounds more complicated than it actually is. All the bank reconciliation does it agree the closing balance per the control account to the balance on the bank statements.

In the previous example, the deposit account shows a nil balance. If it agrees to the bank statement, there is nothing further to do other than note the agreement. However, if there was, say, a small amount of interest on the bank account which you had not recorded then the two would not agree and you would then need to go through and record the bank interest as an additional bank receipt, and reflect this in the income and expenditure account and the balance sheet. The income and expenditure account would then have the extra bank interest received and there would be a balance on the deposit account to reflect the extra income.

Sometimes the control account and the bank account do not agree entirely first time, all the time. When this happens, you will have to go through the bank account and tick the entries in the bank account to the entries in the summary of the bank receipts and payments to see where the differences are. It may be the error in is a difference in recording, so once the amendment is made the balances will agree. If this does not solve the problem, you may have a difference concerning timing issues. This is to say that you may have recorded the cheques received for Lodge subscriptions when they arrive. When cheques are banked within the UK, there is a delay in the banking process. In that when these cheques are then deemed cleared funds in the bank account. As with all UK Banks, they will take up to three days for them to be cleared and available to draw upon. Therefore, it may be that when you try to agree the balances you may need to take account of this delay. Therefore, you have shown the entry as a cheque received but the bank has not yet processed it as cleared funds. This is the timing delay previous referred to. In this instance, you will need to complete a reconciliation showing the reasons for the timing delays. This is explained in Table 19 below.

Table 19

	£
Balance per bank statement at 31.12.20XY	4,207.57
Add outstanding monies received	
Other receipt	1.23
Deduct payments not yet cleared	
Lodge rents	(1,820.00)
Tyler's fee	(10.00)
Closing balance	2,378.80

You can then repeat the above exercise for the various other accounts, and this way you can ensure all entries have been included and nothing omitted. Therefore, the other accounts would appear as indicated in Table 20 opposite.

As you can see, the starting point was the closing figure from the previous year. By adding all the receipts and deducting all the payments for the year, you will have the closing balance. This then agrees to the bank statement. This shows you have included all the receipts you have banked and all the payments you have made. I hope that what you will also observe is that if there is a surplus of income over expenditure it reflects in an increase in the bank account. Therefore, the increase in the balance sheet fund is reflected by the increase in the bank account. The Grand Charity Relief Chest account is actually the clearest example of this.

Table 20

Almoners / Charity Account	
Opening balance	1,023.19
Receipts	3,036.93
Payments	(2,825.00)
Closing balance	1,235.12
Balance per Bank statement	1,235.12
Difference	Nil
Ladies festival account	
Opening balance	556.02
Receipts	8,275.01
Payments	(8,272.72)
Closing balance	558.31
Balance per Bank statement	558.31
Difference	Nil
Grand Charity relief Chest	
Opening balance	7,463.24
Receipts	1,997.50
Payments	(1,500.00)
Closing balance	7,960.74
Balance per Bank statement	7,960.74
Difference	Nil

Payment Procedures

As the Treasurer, you are responsible for paying out as well as collecting the monies due. The payments are usually fewer in number than the receipts, especially for a Lodge where the dining fees are not included within the subscriptions, or are collected by the Lodge and then settled by the Lodge. The majority of the payments will fall under the normal expenditure you incur as a Lodge, such as the hall rent, Grand Lodge Dues, Provincial or Metropolitan Dues and Secretary Expenses. As the Treasurer, you may well have to pay out of the Steward's account at the end of each meeting to settle any outstanding amount for the dinning costs of each meeting, which the Lodge has to cover.

The balance of any payments is likely to be ritual books, Books of Constitution (for the new Initiate), regalia and insurance. These items are under your remit to settle and pay as soon as possible without requiring any additional confirmation from the Lodge, although if they are to be paid by cheque, you will need to present the invoice to one of the other bank signatories, together with your part of the cheque completed for their approval. They will then have the evidence to support what the payment of the cheque is for and provide a second signature to authorise it as a bona fide Lodge expenditure. As the items are within the ordinary purposes of the Lodge you need seek no further confirmation, but what happens if they are not?

The By-Laws of the Lodge should include within them a note providing a stated limit that you are able to settle without needing to refer the payment to the Lodge for approval. You should however, seek out your own Lodge By-Laws, as they may have a sum, which is not suitable in today's monetary value. For example, I have just drafted the first by-Laws for a new lodge, which is being formed, within my Province connected to motor sport, called the Silverstone Lodge 9877. For the new lodge the limit set for the Treasurer to make irregular payments without seeking Lodge approval is £100, which in 2013, appears reasonable. Contrast this with my Mother Lodge, which I was initiated into in 2001 (a mere 12 years earlier) and the limit was set at just £25, which, when the Lodge approved this figure in 1991, it seemed reasonable. Within 10 years this seemed too low, and a further 10 years on seems totally insufficient.

There is a procedure to go through when any item of expenditure exceeds these set limits. You will need to make a notice of motion in one regular meeting and then propose it at the next meeting. It will then need to be seconded and voted on at that next meeting. Then once the vote has been passed by the majority of the brethren, the payment can then be made. So imagine you needed to buy something not deemed to be for the ordinary purpose of the lodge for £50, it could take up to six months to get the payment approved, especially if the Lodge only meets every quarter. Ensuring the limits are regularly reviewed and updated is necessary as Treasurer, as you might be in breach of you by-laws if they are referring to pounds, shillings and pence. It is probably unlikely, but stranger things have happened. In order to change the by-laws to reflect any increase, the secretary will have to give a notice of motion saying he needs to increase the limits. Then at the next meeting have them proposed, seconded and voted on in lodge, and then seek approval from the Provincial or Metropolitan Grand Master before they can the increase can be adopted by the Lodge.

Accruals Accounting

Up until now everything I have explained has been on a simple cash received basis, i.e. recording only those movements, which actually happen. However, you can adopt the accruals accounting method. This is the next step up by accounting for what is due to be received and paid rather than actually received and paid. This is a more complicated method of accounting for the transactions as you have to note what was due to be received and what was actually received, and likewise have a note of what was due to be paid and what was actually paid. The balancing movement will then appear in the balance sheet either as a debtor (people who owe you) or as a creditor (people you owe). The former appears as an asset in the balance sheet above the bank accounts. The creditor is shown as a current liability in a separate part of the balance sheet under the current liabilities heading in the balance sheet. The positioning of this can be seen in the example of a balance sheet in chapter 7. The probable examples of the two main items, which will fall into the need to account for these items, are Lodge subscriptions and dining expenses. Therefore, the best way to illustrate the mechanism for calculating either the debtor or creditor is by way of an example.

For Lodge subscriptions, a Brother can be up to two years in arrears before he is excluded according to the Book of Constitution rule 148. However, your own lodge by-laws may state a shorter period. Therefore, it is possible that in one year you will have outstanding subscriptions. Your accounts should reflect the total amount of the subscriptions due in the year, which if you collect all that is due in that year, would be the case. For example, let us say there are 35 members in the lodge and you have a lodge subscription per member of £150. The total amount of income you will expect to have as income in the accounts is £5,250. Then let us assume that you have expenditure exactly equal to the income of £5,250. However, if two members do not pay the amounts due in the year you will only have received income of £4,950. Let us say that the expenses for the year are exactly equal to the income you expect to receive of £5,250. On a receipts and payments basis, you will have income of £4,950 but expenses of £5,250, which will give you a deficit for the year of £300. (However, you would not have a deficit if the members had paid the subscription in the correct year).

Then if in the following year, you still have the same number of members and the expenses are the same, but the two who did not pay in the previous year have now paid, you will then have income of £5,550 and expenses again of £5,250 and you will have a £300 surplus. Taking the two years together, you have neither a surplus nor a deficit as the two figures are the same, but one year shows a deficit and the other year a surplus. Therefore, the accruals accounting shows the £300 in outstanding subscriptions as a debtor in the first year and nothing in the second year. With each year showing the income as £5,250 and not what was actually received.

It would be the same for any expenses you have not settled. An example of this would be if your Lodge accounts are made up to the 31st December, you always meet on the last day of the month, but you collect the dining fees in and settle the money with the caterers on the following day. Therefore, you have collected 35 meals at £20 per meal and have received £700 in cheques to pay into your bank, wait for them to clear and then you can make the payment to the caterer. However, you cannot bank the cheques until after the bank holiday on the 1st January, and so will not be able to pay the caterers for a few days until the banked the cheques have cleared. Now if you record the dining fees received on the 31st December you have an income of £700 with no expenses to set against it. It then shows you to have a surplus on the dining account, but you do not because you have to settle the outstanding dining fees also of say £700. In order to balance the income and expenditure you need to record the fact that this money needs to be paid out, so you would have to recognise the creditor in the balance sheet and increase the cost of dining fees so there is no surplus shown. These examples are ways of showing the accruals concept of accounting; it is also referred to as the matching concept. So consider it as monies that are matched with the income and expenses to allocate them in the right accounting periods. If this all seems too complicated, then stick with just the receipts and payments accounting and explain any unexpected surpluses or deficits when you present the accounts to members of the Lodge. I will explain this further in chapter 12.

CHAPTER 10

SUBSCRIBING MEMBER'S RECORDS TO KEEP

What is a subscribing member? He is a member of the Lodge who pays his subscriptions annually to the Lodge. The Lodge subscriptions are defined in the Book of Constitutions rule 145 as follows:

> "**145.** All members entitled to the same privileges of a Lodge must pay annually the same amount of subscription, save that, if the by-laws so provide, a smaller rate of annual subscription may be fixed for members who, for some cause satisfactory to the Lodge, are not in a position to enjoy such privileges regularly.
>
> No Lodge may by its by-laws or otherwise provide that any subscribing member thereof shall not be entitled to receive summonses, or be disqualified from holding office therein, but a Lodge may in its by-laws provide that members who are in default in the payment of their subscriptions for some specified period, not less than three months after their becoming due, shall be deprived while so in default of all or any of the rights of voting, proposing or seconding candidates, and being appointed or elected to office."[2]

Therefore, in order to be a member of the Lodge, and take part in the activities of a Lodge, the member must pay his subscriptions. With the role of Treasurer, you need to ensure that you have a record of the subscriptions due, and when they are paid. In effect, you need to maintain a register of the current members and the past members. Keeping the register serves two tasks. The first being that it will give you a list of the monies you are to collect and ensure that all sums due are actually collected. I would also recommend as a control, as well as to ensure completeness that you check to make sure that the total of the bank receipts in the cashbook and the total monies recorded in the register are the same. That way you will know whether you have banked a cheque but left someone on the register as owing dues. The second is to maintain a historic list of the past members who have now left the Lodge. Concerning the past members, the register will maintain the past members details and confirm whether they left in good standing. The definition of good standing is that all Lodge dues are paid up to date. For

---

2   Book of Constitutions, United Grand Lodge of England ©2013

example, if your Lodge financial year runs to December and someone resigns in February without paying his dues, he will not have left in good standing. Likewise, if he has paid he will have left in good standing. Therefore, if he wishes to join a new lodge he will need a clearance certificate, which will show that he was a member of the Lodge and that all his dues were settled. If not then in accordance with rule, 163 (d) of the Book of Constitutions the new Lodge will become liable for his arrears. I have reproduced the rule below for reference. However, if you note that at the time the ballot was taken the secretary can prove that the joining member was not indebted then your lodge will not be liable for his arrears.

> **"Book of Constitution Rule 163 (d)** If a Lodge accepts as a joining member a Brother who has been excluded from a Lodge or who has resigned without having complied with its by-laws or the general regulations of the Craft, it shall be liable for any arrears that may be owing by him to the Lodge or Lodges from which he has been excluded or has resigned. The circumstances of such exclusion or resignation shall be stated to the Lodge before the ballot is taken, the better to enable the Brethren to exercise their discretion as to his admission, but the failure to make such a statement shall not exonerate the Lodge from its liability for such arrears, unless the Secretary shall be able to demonstrate that prior to the ballot he had had produced to him in accordance with paragraph (c) of this Rule a certificate from every Lodge of which the Brother was or had been a member showing that he was not at the time of the ballot indebted thereto."[3]

Therefore, the requirement to maintain detailed records of a member's subscriptions ensures the correct information can be provided to any lodge enquiry you may receive. If any member does leave still owing sums, you should also inform the Provincial Registrar so that the records are updated at that level. Should the Lodge ever have to hand in its Warrant and be erased there will always be a record of a Brother's arrears. Thus making any new Lodge he applies to join aware of his previous non-payment. The format of recording the members and what they have paid and when payment was received has already been illustrated in chapter 3. Please refer back if you want any further indication of the layout.

The only time when you will not have to record subscriptions due will be for those members who are Honorary Members of the Lodge. The detailed requirement of the procedure for electing an Honorary Member is detailed in Rule 167 of the Book of Constitutions. Has been elected as such, he will not be liable to any fees payable to the Lodge. However, he will preserve the right to propose or second members but will not be able to hold an office of the Lodge.

---

3   Book of Constitutions, United Grand Lodge of England ©2013

The reason for collecting in all the outstanding subscriptions is that you will have to pay all fees due to Grand Lodge, Provincial and District Lodges in which the Lodge belongs. You will still have to settle the amounts due to them even if you have not received all sums from the subscribing members. Rule 147 of the Book of Constitutions ensures these must be paid when they are due. When you collect the subscriptions, you may receive them in any form - annual bank transfer, cheque, cash and even direct debit. The main point is that you will need to show the method of payment received from each member in the register.

With the first three methods above, you will only have the one entry to make on the respective line of the members' register. With paying by direct debit, you should record all the dates for each payment received. Therefore, you may wish to include extra lines to accommodate the twelve dates you will have for a member who pays their subscription monthly. Regarding the amounts that they may pay, you might find that most subscriptions are not divisible by twelve, so as we tend to have a subscription calculation rounded to the nearest £5 or £10. I would therefore suggest that they always round up the payments to the nearest whole pound. Any surplus can then be treated as a donation to the lodge, subject to the specific member's approval.

For example, if the annual subscription is £200, when you divide this by 12 it is nearly £16.67 per month. Therefore if rounded up to £17 a month would mean that over the entire year they will pay a total of £204, rather than the amount due of £200. If they agree that this can be donated to the Lodge funds it will make it easier, as otherwise you will have to record a surplus brought forward or refund the difference overpaid to them. In relation to paying by direct debit over a twelve month period, you will have to consider if this would be in breach of any of the by-laws of the Lodge, as, although rule 148 of the Book of Constitutions refers to exclusions for non-payment if they are two years in arrears, your own Lodge may have a different time scale. If you have a by-law, which states that all subscriptions should be paid within six months of the start of the financial year, and a Brother is paying his in equal instalments commencing at the start of the year that would be in breach of the by-law and potentially risk exclusion, if anyone wishes to enforce adherence to the by-law.

I would suggest there are two ways around this. One the by-law is amended to allow the payment of the subscription by a monthly direct debit without the risk of exclusion; or two the Brother or Brothers concerned pay six months in advance. Therefore, if the year starts in January, they will begin to pay in the July of the previous year, and then when the six months has elapsed you will be able to show that the Brother or Brothers are paid up to date. The hope is that during the course of each year you will be able to collect in all the subscriptions due. If however you are unable to do so then the next chapter will guide you through the steps you need to take to exclude a Brother for non-payment should the unfortunate situation arise.

CHAPTER 11

WHAT HAPPENS IF ARREARS ARE BUILT UP?

In the previous chapter, I discussed the collection of Lodge subscriptions. It may take some time to collect all the monies due, and from experience, it may take numerous communications either by telephone calls, emails and personal requests in lodge etc. However, you hope to get all the monies due within the respective periods. In the event that you have been unable to get all dues received, it would be worth talking to any Brother concerned to find out if there is a reason why he has not paid his subscriptions. This chapter deals with the occasions when you have not received all the outstanding dues and every avenue has been exhausted. Rule 148 of the Book of Constitution states:_

Cessation of membership when two years in arrears

"**148.** Should the subscription of a member to his Lodge remain unpaid for two full years, at the expiration of that period he shall cease to be a member of the Lodge, which fact shall be reported to the Lodge at the next regular meeting, and recorded on the minutes. He can only become a member again by regular proposition and ballot according to Rule 163, and the Lodge shall require payment of the arrears as a condition precedent to his election. This Rule shall not prevent any Lodge proceeding against any of its members under Rule 181 in respect of sums due for a shorter period than two years, if so provided in its by-laws. When a Brother ceases to be a member under this Rule, and also when a Brother subsequently pays his arrears of subscription the fact shall be notified to the Grand Secretary and, if the Lodge be within a Metropolitan Area, Province or District, also to the Metropolitan, Provincial or District Grand Secretary. The provisions of Rules 9, 163, 175 and 182 shall apply in the case of a Brother ceasing to be a member under this Rule as if he had been excluded by vote."[4]

The degree of arrears for exclusion may vary from Lodge to Lodge; the above extract from the Book of Constitutions defines it as a period of two years. This is therefore the maximum period in which a member can be in arrears before exclusion can take place. The by-laws of the Lodge may state a shorter period than that shown in rule

---

4   Book of Constitutions, United Grand Lodge of England ©2013

148 above, and in this instance you may need to adhere to the by-laws of the Lodge. The whole purpose of ensuring that all dues are collected is that the Lodge will have to pay all sums due whether the member has paid the subscription or not, so in order to balance up your books you will need to ensure all sums are received. In chapter 13, I will go through in more detail how you will need to calculate a figure for Lodge subscriptions and maintain a balanced set of accounts. This means that you should calculate the subscriptions due on the basis that you will collect payment for all the monies due. Therefore, if you do not collect all the monies due you will have a deficit. The aim is that you will collect in all sums and this will be approximately equal to the amount of monies you are due to pay out.

Concerning the deficit Rule 171 of the Book of Constitutions states that:

Responsibility for fees;
"**171.** A member who proposes or seconds a candidate for initiation or joining membership shall be responsible to the Lodge for all fees payable under its by-laws in respect of such candidate."[5]

This will then mean that the proposer and seconder will then be liable to pay any arrears. I hope that the Brother who has not paid his dues will feel he should pay them to save his proposer and seconder having to. It may also be that the brother in question has fallen on hard times, and it is at this point we should consider the words from our initiation; "........and thirdly, as a warning to your own heart, that should you meet a Brother in distressed circumstances who might solicit your assistance, you will remember the peculiar moment you were received into Freemasonry, poor and penniless, and cheerfully embrace the opportunity of practising that virtue you have professed to admire."[6] If the Brother has not paid his subscriptions for the required period and you have made all attempts to try to recover the arrears but have failed then you will have to consider permanent exclusion. The main thought behind exclusion is that if a Brother is continually failing to pay his dues by choice rather than circumstance then he will have to be subsidised by the rest of the Brethren in the Lodge. I would always see the use of Rule 181 as a last attempt, but unfortunately, sometimes it cannot be avoided. I think it is for this reason that the procedures are laid out in a chronological order and with specific steps to be taken.

"**181. (a)** Any Lodge may by resolution exclude any member for sufficient cause, provided that
(i) a notice in writing shall have been served upon him by Registered Post, the envelope being plainly marked on the outside 'Private and

---

5   Book of Constitutions, United Grand Lodge of England ©2013

6   Emulation Ritual

Confidential', not less than fourteen days before the meeting at which the complaint is to be considered, together with particulars of the complaint made against him, stating the time and place appointed for the meeting and that he may attend to answer the complaint in person or make answer in writing if he prefers.

(ii) not less than ten days' notice in writing shall also have been served on the members of the Lodge of the intention to propose such a resolution.

(b) The notices shall be considered duly served if sent by post to the last known address of each member.

(c) The name of the Brother concerned shall not appear in the notice served upon the members of the Lodge, but must be made known to the Brethren when the resolution is moved at the meeting.

(d) The voting shall be by ballot.

(e) The resolution shall not be carried unless two-thirds of the members present vote in favour of it.

(f) If the resolution is carried, the exclusion shall be effective forthwith.

(g) The name of every Brother excluded from a Lodge, with the cause of the exclusion, shall forthwith be sent to the Grand Secretary and, if the Lodge be within a Metropolitan Area, Province or District, also to the Metropolitan, Provincial or District Grand Secretary.

(h) When the cause of exclusion is non-payment of subscriptions for a period shorter than that prescribed in Rule 148 (if so provided in the Lodge's by-laws), the Grand Secretary, and if the Lodge be within a Metropolitan Area, Province or District, the Metropolitan, Provincial or District Grand Secretary shall be notified if the Brother concerned subsequently pays the arrears of subscription.

(j) In this Rule to "exclude" a Brother means to terminate the Brother's membership of the Lodge, and the terms "exclude", "excluded", and "exclusion" shall be construed accordingly.

N.B. the term expelled is used only where a Brother is removed from the Craft by the Grand Lodge"[7]

If it finally does come down to exclusion then the exact steps of Rule 181 of the Book of Constitutions must be followed.

---

7   Book of Constitutions, United Grand Lodge of England©2013

CHAPTER 12

PRESENTATION OF ANNUAL ACCOUNTS

Now that your first year as Lodge Treasurer has finished, you have prepared the accounts and the Auditors have reviewed them and agreed that all is in order. You will then have to present the accounts to the rest of the Lodge. This gives the members of the Lodge the opportunity to raise any questions. Once the accounts have been approved, the Lodge can adopt them. The aim of this chapter is to give some guidance on presenting the accounts and delivering a statement, which ensures the Lodge, agrees upon the accounts. In relation to the audit requirements, I will explain this in chapter 14.

When it comes to presenting the accounts, you will need to stand up in the lodge and address the brethren. I would suggest that you draft a report and deliver it to the brethren. It does not have to be a lengthy report, as by the time you are presenting the accounts it is usually one of the latter items on the agenda for that meeting. Rule 153 of the Book of Constitutions states that you need to produce a set of accounts annually, which shows the financial position of the accounts under the name of the lodge. This will include all the accounts and funds as previously described. The term financial position refers to the snap shot in time of all the accounts and it is more commonly the balance sheet date of the lodge. This shows all the bank balances and (if adopted) the assets and liabilities of the lodge. What I hope you will have understood is that the difference in this year's balance sheet and the previous one is the surplus or deficit made during the year. Think of it as last year's balance sheet being the start of the journey and this year's balance sheet the end of the journey, with the income and expenditure account being the summarised movements of how you got there. If you make a large surplus or deficit in the year, you will expect a significant change to be reflected in the bank balance at the year-end.

The rule goes on to state that the books and records should be available to the Brethren for inspection at the meeting they are presented. This is to ensure transparency of your work. It is also suggested that the audited accounts will be sent out to all members with the summons prior to the meeting at which the accounts will be presented. This will make it easier for any Brother to ask a question to you prior to the meeting. The rules in the Book of Constitutions go on to set the date at which the accounts should be presented to the members of the lodge. It says that accounts should not be presented to the Brethren any later than the third meeting from the date the accounts are made up to, this means that if your accounts finish in December, and you meet every month you will need to present them by the March meeting. If the meetings are further apart then you will have a longer period to present them. Do not be afraid to state what might appear to be obvious, as not all people understand accounts. Being an accountant, I always thought they were self-explanatory but that is because I have prepared and read many sets of accounts. If you have changed any of the formats of the accounts to reflect the schedules in this book you might wish to explain why. As with all things, the reason for a change might be for the best, but there may be resistance to it from all, especially if they have been a member of the Lodge for a long time and used to seeing the accounts in the old format. The main reason you would make any changes to the accounts is to make sure that the accounts are more readable and understandable for all members. Additionally you may well be including new accounts for separate funds, which have not previously been included.

The items I would mention in any report would be:

- If all Lodge subscriptions have been collected.
- Comment upon any particular increase in expenses and explain why.
  - ☐ E.g., the regalia costs are higher as we have purchased three Past Master jewels, etc.
- Comment upon the net surplus or deficit on a particular account for the year, explaining why it has happened and whether any additional steps need to be taken concerning preventing the surplus or deficit from happening again.
  - ☐ E.g., there has been a large payment out to a charity/festival from the Relief Chest account, which you have been saving towards for a number of years.
- The solvency of the Lodge accounts, i.e. how much money is in the accounts and how you have managed the expenses from month to month.
- If any delay in collecting subscriptions has caused delays in settling accounts or fees payable by the Lodge.
- You may wish to state the purpose of each fund, and why you have the funds shown separately.
- There may have been considerable sums spent by the Steward's at the festive board and state what affects this has had on the Lodge subscriptions.
- If there is a potential need to increase the Lodge subscriptions due to current spending levels (I will go through the procedures for increasing subscriptions in the next chapter).

Remember there is nothing in the Book of Constitutions, which states you have to answer the questions raised in open Lodge, especially if you feel the question would take a long time to answer or may be a particularly sensitive topic to a brother in the Lodge. If this is the case, it may be that you defer answering the question until a later meeting after speaking with the parties concerned. However, you will need to present the answer in open lodge as the question was asked in open lodge, thus ensuring all Brethren are able to hear the answer. It may also be necessary for the Brother who asked the question to get up at the subsequent meeting and withdraw either the question or state that it has been resolved to his personal satisfaction on anything of a personal nature, which may be sensitive to a Brother in the Lodge. However, in my own experience of being a Lodge Treasurer, it is unusual to be asked a question. You just need to remember that the option is there for questions to be raised. You may wish to produce a supporting schedule of any items that may have questions raised prior to the accounts being presented. That way you will have everything prepared and an explanation ready for the meeting.

CHAPTER 13

CALCULATING PER CAPITA FEES FOR LODGE SUBSCRIPTIONS TO COVER OUTGOINGS

This chapter might also have been called 'balancing up the books', as I am hopefully going to lay out the mechanics of working out what your Lodge subscription figure might be. As this is your main source of income to cover the majority of the expenses it is an important calculation.

The best way to look at balancing up the Lodge accounts is with a simple analogy. If your annual income is two thousand pounds and you spend one thousand nine hundred and ninety nine pounds you will be happy, but if you have the same two thousand pound income, but spend two thousand and one pound you will have to fund the deficit from somewhere. It might be that this comes from a previous surplus brought forward, but eventually this surplus will run out, and you will have a problem. So therefore, if you can balance the books you will succeed. The aim of this chapter is to explain basic calculations to cover your core and variable costs each year.

If you take over from an existing Treasurer, you will have some historical information that you can use in order to assess if the calculation of Lodge subscriptions is set at the right level. When I took over from the previous Treasurer in my Lodge, I discovered that our costs to Grand Lodge, Provincial Lodge and Hall rents exceeded our Lodge subscription by £3 per member. It does not sound like a lot but we had no contribution towards any of the other costs the Lodge incurred such as the festive board, secretary expenses, regalia costs and Lodge insurance etc. It did make me unpopular with the Lodge that as soon as I took over I had to increase the Lodge subscriptions by a large amount to cover the annual deficit the Lodge was incurring. I feel that part of the problem may have been down to the way the accounts were laid out as horizontal account formats rather than vertical account formats. At no point did the accounts show a surplus or a deficit, which would have enabled the more senior Brethren to raise the issue and address it. The other part of the problem was the reluctance of the Treasurer to increase the subscriptions. Unfortunately, whilst it may make you unpopular, you have to do what is needed for the good of the Lodge. If this means upsetting some Lodge members for the good of the Lodge, it still needs to be done. In these circumstances, you need to have the tools to calculate what the subscriptions need to be to cover all the expenses. During the course of this book, I have shown various examples to illustrate the work needed to calculate the correct subscription level.

When you look at the income and expenditure account of the worked example, you will see it shows a small surplus of £158.67 for the year. So at first glance, it would appear that the lodge subscriptions are set at the right level. However, this is not actually the case. When you review the bank receipts analysis in chapter 4 the total amount of subscriptions received for the year was £3,000, but this is broken down into all the subscriptions for the current year of £2,880 and one from the previous year of £120. Therefore, the surplus for this year of £158.67 is actually only a surplus for this year of £38.67, as £120 was carried forward from the previous year. The next thing to consider is that you have other types of income, which are actually supplementing the total income and effectively contributing to the core costs. For example, if there was money raised at a summer BBQ of £159.94 and a donation of £125.00. These two items would total £284.94. Therefore, what first appears to be a successful set of accounts is actually running at a deficit of £246.27. If there are no other items of income, then we have a Lodge, which is running at a large deficit per annum. If you look at the expenses and divide this by the number of members in the Lodge, you end up with a shortfall. I would layout my calculations as follows in Table 21.

Table 21

My Lodge Accounts number XXXX
Projected position for the lodge year 31st December 20XY
Budget

Per Capita fees	Total	Members		Per member	
Grand Lodge dues	952.00	24	=	39.67	
Lodge rent	1,820.00	24	=	75.83	
Provincial Grand Lodge	224.00	24	=	9.33	
					124.83
General expenses					
Secretary expenses	32.22	24	=	1.34	
Ritual & regalia	10.00	24	=	0.42	
Insurance	70.00	24	=	2.92	
Tyler fees	80.00	24	=	3.33	
Sundries	5.98	24	=	0.25	
Xmas Gratuities and gifts	40.00	24	=	1.67	
					9.93
Projected spend per head					134.76

Current dues	120.00
estimated spend per head	134.76
Shortfall per head	(14.76)
Shortfall for the year based on members	(501.78)

As you can see the accounts do not look as good as they first appear. With the example of the accounts used, they show a small surplus. This however takes into account the other income received for the year. As you can see from the above calculation, there is a shortfall. In this instance, you would have to increase the lodge subscriptions to at least £135 per member to cover expenses for the year, if you excluded the other income. The breakdown of the costs incurred falls into two types, the first being the per capita costs and the others being the general costs.

To explain the differences between them you need to appreciate that the per capita fees are the same whether you have 100 members or just 10, as these are member specific. Therefore, this becomes a variable cost on the number of members. In the above example, you can see that the costs of all of these expenses are more than the actual subscriptions collected. The total variable costs are £124.83 per member and yet the subscription fee is only £120.00. Therefore, you have a deficit of £4.83 per member before any other costs. The other expenses are a mixture of fixed and variable expenses. The fixed cost of the insurance is the same whether you have 100 or 10 members. This would mean that the cost to each member would be 70p or £7 depending on having either 100 or 10 members. Therefore, if your lodge numbers are declining you should consider the fixed costs in reference to the subscriptions. Some of the other costs are variable, for example if you are all on email and the summons is sent out electronically then your costs for the secretary will be reduced, but if the Brethren all receive the summons by post, then the Secretary's costs will be higher and also dependent upon the numbers of members in the Lodge.

In my Province, it is normal practice to have a reduced meal price at the festive board for any visiting Masters from a Sister Lodge. This means depending on the meal you can end up with a cost to be met by the Lodge in relation to each meal. This means the more visiting masters a lodge has at each meeting the greater the cost will be for the steward's account at the end of the year. This again will consume the funds available each year. Therefore, this will need to be considered in your subscription calculation. The only advantage you will have is that you can refer to historical figures to assess the expected costs each year for visiting masters. Reviewing the previous year's accounts is a useful place to start when looking into the calculation of the correct subscription level. These will give you an indication of the past costs and which you can compare this with the per capita fees which you will receive prior notification of from Grand Lodge. You can then work out the correct level of subscription needed for the forth-coming year. The other costs of the Lodge are known. However, you might need to consider including a small sum for unexpected costs, but in general terms this should only be a small figure.

The above example is set out for a Lodge, which does not include dining fees in the subscriptions. As some Lodges are dining Lodges, we should also consider this. With most Lodges, not all of the members attend every meeting, and depending on the number of attendees, it would then depend on how you calculate the dining costs. In the example, we have 24 members, and the Lodge meets eight times a year. Therefore, if the cost of each meal is £20 for eight meetings, for all 24 members the cost of dining will be £3,840 a year or an extra £160 per member. However, if you only have an attendance of 16 members on average for each meeting you will have a meal cost of £2,560. This means there would be an extra £1,280 collected each year from the members but with no dining expenses incurred. You will need to review the subscriptions to consider this. However, you will never be able to know who will and will not be dining for the entire year. There may be other dining costs you will need to pay for during each year due to official guests or contributing visitor's meals.

The other option may be to assume that you do not see all the members each year and estimate that you may only see 16. This would then bring down the subscriptions for all members from an extra £160 per member to £106.67. This is calculated as the total dining fees of £2,560 divided by the number of members. This would be suitable, but what happens if the number dining on average throughout the year rises to 20. You would have a serious shortfall in the dining costs for that year. I would therefore suggest that the best action is to review the historic dining costs collected with the dining costs paid in the previous year to see if you have calculated the figure correctly. You must also consider the changing profile of the Lodge. It may be you are now seeing more of the previous unseen Brethren or vice versa. It might even be worth discussing it with the other members of the Lodge, but always go equipped with any calculations to support what you think is the best level of subscription and why.

I used the above template when I needed to increase the subscriptions when I took over as Treasurer in my Lodge. I showed that we could not carry on spending more than we were receiving, and demonstrated it by using the above template. It showed clearly, why I needed to increase the Lodge subscriptions and what figure they should be. There is a procedure for increasing the subscriptions. Before they are due you will need to have a vote in open Lodge to increase them, and it will need to appear on the summons. In order for it to appear on the summons, you need to give a notice of motion at the meeting prior. This means that if the Lodge subscriptions are due in January and you only meet 4 times a year in January, March, September and November, you would need to give a notice of motion at the September meeting and have it appear on the summons for November so that it can be voted on in Lodge at the November meeting. This will then enable you to increase the subscriptions for collection in January.

When preparing the calculation of the breakeven position for the Lodge subscription you should also consider what is to be paid out. So far, we have accepted the costs incurred and fixed the income to cover these costs. In the majority of the accounts, you will find there is not much chance of reducing costs. For example, if you wanted to consider reducing the monies you pay to Grand Lodge you would have no option but to pay the sums requested. It is written in the Book of Constitution that they must be paid. However, you can look at the other costs and assess if these can be reduced. It might be that the Stewards always put out a bottle of wine for each visiting Master and at the end of each night, two thirds is thrown away, as they may be driving home after the festive board. It might be that there is always a glass of port for each member at the Lodge's expense, but if this equates to a substantial expense over the year then it may be necessary look to see if this can be cut out. If this has always been a traditional expense in the Lodge, it would be highly unlikely that you will be able to stop it without some resistance, but you must make the members aware of how much of their subscription is going on port. It might be it is put to a vote in the Lodge, especially if a minority only enjoys the port.

With the advent of email communication, it is now possible to circulate the summons to the members electronically, and with the price of stamps increasing, this could represent a significant saving. For example, the current cost of a first class stamp is 60p, so for our 24 members for the eight meetings the cost of postage is £115.20 or £4.80 per member. Change the method of distribution to electronic means and this will effectively save £5 on the Lodge subscription. Controlling the costs is a fundamental part of the office you have accepted. It is best to have an inquiring mind and ask 'should we continue to do this?', and if the answer comes back "well it is what we have always done it", then you will know there is no reason not to seek change. If we all carried on the way Lodges first started we would all live within the length of our cable tow to the Lodge and have to walk to each meeting, as our ancestors never drove, because the car had not yet been invented. The final part to consider with the calculation of the Lodge subscription is whether you have any country members. This might be a new term, but effectively it means you have members who do not attend regularly and pay a different level of subscription.

From the above examples, it should be clear to see how to calculate the subscriptions payable for the normal costs and those members that pay for the normal costs and dining fees. Therefore, a full subscription to include dining fees would be £280 (The current subscription of £120 plus dining fees of £160) whereas the country members would only pay the £120. On the worked example earlier in the chapter, I showed that the other income was contributing to the overall cost of the membership, so if you then applied this increase to this summary then the subscriptions would be £295 & £135 respectively. This in part settles some of the queries concerning setting the level of subscriptions for dining members and those that do not normally dine. The method of calculating the country members and normal members subscriptions is a little bit more complicated, especially as the costs in our example shows that the full subscription does cover the cost of fees payable to Grand Lodge, Provincial or Metropolitan and the Hall rents. The only point a country member could make is that they are not using the Hall, and therefore why should they pay the hall rent. However, if the hall were levying the rents based on the numbers of members, the shortfall would have to be paid by the other members. Is this fair or just what has always been done? As mentioned in chapter 10 setting the subscription levels for those who pay a different level of subscription should enjoy a reduced level of privileges. This is covered in rule 145 of the book of constitutions.

Personally, I would only advocate a reduced subscription if it included dining fees and a Brother lives so far away that attendance is not regularly permitted. However, in this instance you are reducing their involvement according to the Book of Constitutions, unless your By-Laws permit it. You may therefore consider removing the meal costs from the subscriptions and make the members pay for their meals on the night. In order to show how you might work out a different level of subscription for country members, I have included an example below, working based on three members not attending regularly and already enjoying the country membership. I have excluded the dining aspect as I hope that this is self-explanatory as shown in Table 22.

Table 22

My Lodge Accounts number XXXX

Projected position for the lodge year 31st December 20XY

Budget

Per Capita fees	Total	Full Members	Country Members		Per Full Member	Per Country Member
Grand lodge dues	952.00	21	3	=	39.67	39.67
Lodge rent	1,820.00	21	3	=	86.67	N/A
Provincial grand lodge	224.00	21	3	=	9.33	9.33
					135.67	49.00
General expenses						
Secretary expenses	32.22	21	3	=	1.34	1.34
Ritual & regalia	10.00	21	3	=	0.42	0.42
Insurance	70.00	21	3	=	2.92	2.92
Tyler fees	80.00	21	3	=	3.33	3.33
Sundries	5.98	21	3	=	0.25	0.25
Xmas Gratuities and gifts	40.00	21	3	=	1.67	1.67
					9.93	9.93
Projected spend per head					145.59	58.93

Therefore, you can see that because of the country members reduced subscriptions each of the full member's subscription needs to increase by £10.83 to cover the costs not shared by the country members. As previously stated this might be considered unfair, and if the Brethren were aware of the different level of subscription, it might cause a problem. However, if it has always been done that way and there is no way to change it then, hopefully, the template illustrates the basis of the calculation. All I have done is to divide all the costs by the total membership, with the exception of the hall rents which I have only divided the total amount due by the full members. This gives the different levels of subscriptions of say £145 for a full member and £60 for a country member.

If you do take away the dining fees from the subscription you will need to ensure that the costs are controlled to prevent these from contributing to the deficit for the year. In essence, the best way I have found to control the costs is to ensure all Brethren who have booked into dine, pay for the meals you have been charged for, even if they do not attend. They have booked in so they pay. You may also wish to restrict the amount of free wine you supply, this way you can minimise the outgoings. I have drafted a format for you to use to ensure all monies are collected and so at the end of the evening you will know what is due to be paid from Lodge funds for dining costs. In fact, when I was the Senior Steward I would reconcile the bill for presentation to the Lodge Treasurer. To illustrate this, if all meals are paid for and there were three visiting Masters whose meals had been subsidised by the lodge at £5 each and they had a bottle of wine between them at a cost of £10, I could show exactly why I needed £25 from Lodge funds to settle the bill for the evening. It does seem a little precise, but was very helpful in ascertaining and accurately recording the outlay. Therefore, ask the same from your Senior Steward when the evening is over. All of the above is a way to achieve the sentiments from the beginning this chapter to ensure you do not spend more than you collect in.

CHAPTER 14

LODGE AUDITORS PROGRAMME - WHAT YOU NEED TO PROVIDE AND WHAT THEY NEED TO DO

At each installation meeting a new set of Lodge Auditors are elected in open Lodge. They are proposed and seconded and then their appointment is voted upon, however, what are the criteria for their election. Some Provinces refer to Lodge examiners not auditors, as an audit is a term used in commercial accounting and is restricted to larger companies, which is an expression upon the truth and fairness of the company accounts, more commonly referred to as being materially correct. Materially correct can be explained as nearly correct, but within accepted tolerances. However, an examiner reviews the transactions and confirms this to the members of the Lodge. In essence an audit, but avoiding the implications of the term audit. Therefore, if your Province uses the term examiner, then substitute examiner for auditor. Grand Lodge refers to the review of a set of accounts by the auditor, so I have adopted this term to cover this section.

When I was a Junior Deacon, and having only been a member of my Lodge for a short time, I was one of the elected auditors, as it was the usual tradition in my Lodge at that time that the Junior and Senior Deacon in office were to be appointed as the Lodge Auditors. From my own experience, I was aware of what was needed to audit large companies, but not a set of Lodge accounts. With my background I carried out the usual checks I considered necessary, such as the bank balances agreed to the accounts, invoices supported all cheques paid out and all Lodge subscriptions had been collected. As this to me at the time seemed to be the extent of what was required. However, several years on, I know that I should have considered more items. It has now been advised in the latest quarterly communication from Grand Lodge (March 2013) that only senior members of the Lodge should carry out the audit, unless you have a junior member with a significant knowledge of accountancy or bookkeeping. This makes sense, as how can a junior member of the Lodge have an understanding of the rules and regulations within the Book of Constitutions regarding the accounts? Even if they have read the rules, they may not have been able to apply these to the lodge accounts. Therefore, when I became the Treasurer of my Lodge, I looked into what I should and should not do concerning preparing the accounts, and it was a natural progression from there to look at what auditors should be looking for when carrying out the Lodge audit. It struck me that if I did not know exactly what I should be considering when appointed as Lodge Auditor how many others did not know what needed to be done either?

In normal company audits we have a programme to follow to ensure all points are considered. It therefore made sense to me that we should also have a lodge audit programme, serving two purposes; the first giving a checklist for any auditor to work through and secondly to make sure all aspects of the Lodge accounts were thoroughly checked through before reporting to the Lodge members. I have reproduced my own suggested audit programme in Table 23, and will clarify each item.

Table 23
Audit programme for lodge auditors

	Test agreed (Yes /No/Not Applicable)
1. Are all subscriptions paid in the year? If not, have any been outstanding for more than two years (or a shorter period as per your by-laws) and if so should the member be considered for exclusion?(Book of Constitution 148)	
2. Have all subscriptions been banked without undue delay?	
3. Has clearance been obtained from the HM Revenue & Customs not to return the income received on bank accounts? If not, has the CT600 been completed and submitted?	
4. Do the lodge accounts include all bank accounts and funds in the name of the lodge, including General account, Charity/Almoners/ Benevolent account, Ladies Festival or Steward's account and Relief Chest account (Book of Constitutions 153)? If not these should now be included.	
5. Have all alms collections been agreed to the lodge minutes and banked without undue delay?	
6. Are there at least two cheque signatories for the cheque books and have all cheques been signed by at least the treasurer and one other member who was approved in open lodge?	
7. If electronic payments have been made, was the authority for the treasurer to make these payments approved in open lodge? If not, authority should now be obtained and consideration of the payments made to check if payments were correctly paid out.	
8. Do the lodge accounts include all receipts and payments for the year? Where considered necessary check the payments made against the invoices.	
9. Do the closing bank balances in the accounts agree to the bank statements after making any allowances for outstanding items of either cheques paid or receipts banked? Review the bank reconciliations	

	Test agreed (Yes /No/Not Applicable)
10. Is the general fund expenditure covered by the lodge subscriptions, or is there a deficit which will require an increase in lodge subscriptions or a large surplus which would enable a reduction?	
11. Have all of the Grand Lodge dues been paid on time? If paid more than 6 months after the due date, Grand Lodge has the power of erasure of a lodge or lesser penalty (Book of Constitution 152).	
12. Are all monies received allocated to their correct purpose? If there are several funds can a breakdown be obtained to ensure no fund is mixed with another?	
13. Bank interest received is subject to tax under the treatment of an unincorporated association under Section 832 of the Income & Corporation Taxes Act 1988. If bank interest received is significant consider the need for this to be returned to HM Revenue & Customs on a Form CT600.	
14. Do all the bank accounts, debtors, investments and creditors equal the balance on the retained funds for the year? (Thus confirming that all items have been included).	
15. If all the above are Yes, the auditor statement should be signed to approve the accounts. If not, outstanding items will need to be addressed.	

I will now explain in more detail each of the above questions

Point 1

This point is to ensure that all Lodge subscriptions have been paid up to date and that no Brother is in arrears. The Book of Constitution states that the arrears should not be in excess of two years overdue, although Lodge By-Laws may specify a different period. In this instance, you should refer to the Lodge By-Laws. If the subscriptions are past the due collection date then the Auditor should ask the Treasurer why he has not moved to exclude the Brother in accordance with the lodge by-laws.

Point 2

Rule 153 of the Book of Constitutions states that all monies should be deposited by the treasurer without undue delay. This has been left undefined in order to give some flexibility. The important point to note is "undue", as the treasurer may not bank the cheques for three weeks but if he has been on holiday for three weeks then the delay is reasonable. Therefore, with this item you will have to apply common sense and reason to any delay.

Point 3

A Lodge is treated as a non-trade association for corporation tax and as such, it is not liable for tax on the subscriptions collected and likewise it does not claim the expenses as a deduction from assessable income. However, if there is bank interest received and other investment income this is liable to corporation tax at the lower rate, which at present is 20%. Now in most instances the HMRC will issue a clearance notice saying that they do not want to receive tax returns each year as the total income and tax raised is not cost effective to collect. Therefore, the Treasurer should have a letter from HMRC stating this. The Auditor would need to ask to see the notice to confirm, as the penalty for failing to return a corporation tax return CT600 is currently £100 if not completed within 12 months of the end of the accounting year. Then after this date, the penalties continue to increase.

Point 4

The Treasurer should report annually on all the accounts that bear the name of the Lodge in the account name, and this should include all the accounts. Quite often, some accounts are forgotten about and the auditor will need to ask if there are any missing accounts. When reviewing other Lodge accounts the one most often forgotten about is the Charity Relief Chest administered by the Grand Charity.

Point 5

The Auditor will be able to check that the alms collected in open Lodge are the same as those recorded in the minutes kept by the secretary, and differences will need to be investigated and resolved.

Point 6

There should be at least two (if not three) cheque signatories authorised by the Lodge to sign the cheques. The Treasurer and one other signatory must sign all cheques. Therefore, the Auditor needs to enquire what the cheque signing procedure is for your Lodge. If this includes one of the members of the Lodge authorised to sign cheques who just signs a selection of blank cheques for the Treasurer to complete when he needs, then the control of having all Lodge cheques signed by two members of the Lodge fails completely. A blank signed cheque can be written out for whatever purpose the other signatory wants with no double check. This should not happen.

Point 7

With the advent of electronic payments, a Lodge Treasurer can use this method to pay for items on behalf of the Lodge; this then contradicts the previous point. Therefore, you need two cheque signatories but the Treasurer can pay out all the items he wants electronically without need for secondary verification. This can only happen when approved by the Lodge members, and it might be that when such approval is sought it is also restricted to a monetary amount for non-regular items and/or particular types of expenditure, such as dining fees, Provincial and Grand Lodge fees, etc. If this procedure has been adopted, then the Lodge committee should consider it.

Point 8
Has everything been included? Look to see if there are any omissions with items of expenses and do the summary of Lodge subscriptions received from the members register agree to the total amount of subscriptions banked. Also, consider looking at any item of expenditure to see if it agrees to an authorised invoice.

Point 9
Do the balances shown on the bank statements at the year-end date agree to the accounts? If they do not, are these reconciled to show why there is a difference? It may be that cheques written have yet to be presented, or cheques received have been recorded but not banked at the year-end date.

Point 10
Are the monies collected annually from the Lodge subscriptions sufficient to cover the actual and expected running costs of the Lodge? If not are there specific reasons? I know of one Lodge where surplus funds have been accumulated over a number of years, and the senior members of the Lodge have taken a deliberate decision to keep the Lodge subscriptions low in order to utilise some of the surplus funds accumulated. Likewise, I know of another Lodge where it has no surplus and needs all the monies due plus some from Lodge funds to maintain the Lodge's finances.

Point 11
This is a simple point, have all monies due to Grand Lodge been paid on time, as if not the repercussions can be serious for the Lodge.

Point 12
When monies other than subscriptions are received, they are for a specific purpose, and the Lodge Auditors need to ensure that all the monies are allocated to the correct fund. For example, you had a substantial donation left to the Lodge by a member of, say, £10,000, but this money was left to the Lodge to benefit specifically, any member of the Lodge in distressed circumstances. The donation was banked in the general fund with all the other monies, then it may be that at some point in the future a new Lodge Treasurer looks at the general fund and seeing it has a significant balance, that may suggest reducing the

Lodge subscriptions to utilise the excess money in the account. This would mean that should a Brother in distressed circumstances come to the Lodge seeking assistance, the fund might have been depleted unintentionally. Therefore, monies received for specific purposes need to be designated as such in the accounts.

Point 13

Bank interest and other investment income received is liable to corporation tax, the auditor will need to ensure that the appropriate forms are completed and submitted to the HMRC, unless point 3 applies.

Point 14

Does the balance sheet show all the assets and liabilities of the Lodge and does this agree to the monies held on the particular fund brought forward (after making due allowances for any surplus or deficit in the year). For further detail on the format of the balance sheet, please refer back to chapter 7.

Point 15

Once all the above points have been satisfactorily agreed upon by the Lodge Auditors they can sign off the report appended to the accounts stating that they have agreed all matters to be satisfied and that the Lodge accounts are all in order.

The format of the report will probably not differ from the one in the previous year's accounts. There is no specific wording laid down within Rule 153 of the Book of Constitutions. However, I have included an example below which I use on the accounts I present to my lodge should you want one for a reference.

When it comes to the Lodge audit, being carried out you will need to ensure that all spreadsheets have been printed out for reference, all bank statements and building society passbooks are available for the entire year and all invoices paid out during the year are available for inspection. It might be that all invoices need to be verified in full, or a sample be selected. That will depend upon the Lodge Auditors being carried out. You should also have all correspondence with the HMRC available for inspection, as well as completed tax forms if applicable. The circulated minutes should also be present so that any income or expenses noted in them can be verified as moving in or out of the bank account as necessary. Cheque books and paying in books should also be available as well as the member's register to agree the subscription dates and amounts. If there is any significant investment in the accounts then appropriate documentation should be available for inspection to support those items. It may be that your Lodge owns the building, in this instance it might be worth having the title deeds checked. This can be done on line at http://www.landregistry.gov.uk/

Example of Lodge Audit Report

We the undersigned, having been appointed as Auditors of the Lodge, confirm that we have made due enquiry into the books and records maintained by the Treasurer on behalf of the Lodge in accordance with Rule 153 of the Book of Constitutions and confirm that the balances held have been duly verified and agreed and that the income and expenditure accounts duly reflect the movements for the lodge funds for the year stated.

.... Auditor .... Auditor

The only point to consider with this would be that a Masonic Lodge is not a strict legal entity and therefore cannot hold property in its own name. The property might be registered to a selection of individuals who may or may not belong to the Lodge. They may hold it as Nominees on behalf of the Lodge, but it would never hurt to check what is actually recorded. The property might be owned by a limited company and the Lodge has control over the shares in that company, which actually solves some of the problem, as a limited company is a legal entity capable of owning property, .

I hope this has clarified the work that an Auditor of the Lodge should carry out. I do not believe that when any Brother takes on the role of Lodge Auditor he truly appreciates his responsibilities to the Lodge. It is an important appointment as it calls on the Brothers to ensure that all is being correctly accounted for and that the accounts agree to the underlying records. A Masonic Lodge is not usually complex and as such the majority of audits carried out will be very straightforward and the accounts will reflect that.

The audit should always be reflective of the size and complexity of a set of accounts, so if it is straight forward, a simple procedure can be adopted. If it is more complex, your lodge will have to hope that you have a couple of accountants in the lodge that can carry out the appointed office to the satisfaction of the members of the lodge. Also, if all else fails, you can always seek guidance and support from the Provincial or District Treasurer, who is likely to be an accountant. Finally, I hope this illustrates why Grand Lodge recommends that Lodge Auditors are more senior members of the Lodge as the office they have been appointed to have many responsibilities resting upon it.

CHAPTER 15

COMPLEX TAX AND ACCOUNTING ISSUES TO CONSIDER

During the first part of this book, I have covered the basics of Lodge accounts. You will also need a basic understanding of the more detailed aspects of Lodge accounts and the respective issues of dealing with the H M Revenue & Customs in relation to aspects of the taxation you will encounter. The only point I would make is that with the ever-evolving aspects of taxation you should seek specific advice for any complex matter.

The aspects for this chapter are:

- Legal status
- Trading activities for Masonic halls (including VAT aspects)
- Concept of mutuality
- Corporation tax
    - ☐ Filing returns & iXBRL & pdf's
    - ☐ Types of income
    - ☐ New Lodge set up
- Capital Gains Tax
- Dealing with Tax Authorities
- Gift Aid

Legal Status

For tax purposes a Lodge is a special form of unincorporated association or members club, and as such all the assets belong to the members of the Lodge. However, English Law does not permit the ownership of assets by more than four people. In this sense, it was impossible until just recently for a partnership to own assets. The assets had always been recorded as belonging to the partners, up to the maximum of four. The recent developments and the creations of Limited Liability Partnerships gave them a legal status, and as such, they were then capable of being able to hold assets in their own name. Therefore as most lodges were consecrated prior to this it would be fair to assume that the assets are recorded as belonging to individuals on behalf of the Lodge. This might need to be reviewed with any substantial assets which may be in the names of former members no longer in the lodge.

Trading Activities for Masonic Halls

The majority of Lodges operate out of buildings used by a collection of Lodges and other side degrees. The property would normally be owned by a limited company, in which Lodges, or an entire Province or District owns the shares of that company. This then gets around the issue of ownership by more than four people as the property is owned by a legal entity (the limited company) and the various Lodges and even the Province or District owns the shares in that limited company. In fact, in Northampton our Masonic Centre is owned by a limited company, which was incorporated in 1888.

There may be a few Lodges, which have their own building and as such will be responsible for all aspects of it. If the Lodge owns a property in its own right, the responsibility of its ownership will be dedicated to the trustees who are the named parties on the documents. What are the duties of the Trustees? It may be looked upon as a favourable office to hold, but in reality, it becomes an office of convenience. The office will then rotate through the various nominated individuals. However, as the nominated individual, they will be responsible to the Lodge for the stewardship of the building. They will need to consider the financial situation of the Lodge including special care being taken to the upkeep and maintenance of the building. There may even be a separate management committee set up to cover any additional expenditure or maintenance. With many Lodge buildings dating back many years, it will be inevitable that over the course of time the building will continue to need routine maintenance and every so often might require substantial maintenance.

In this instance, it might be better to show the expenditure as a separate fund in the accounts, thus showing what level of expenditure is allocated to maintaining the building. If you are fortunate enough to have a surplus of cash as a Lodge, you should ask a Brother suitably trained for his opinion on the current condition of the building.

For example, if everything is at an acceptable level at the present point in time, but it might be that you anticipate a significant cost looming in the not too distance future, you would be better to allocate some funds each year to a building and maintenance fund. Then when the substantial repair bill arrives, there are funds available to cover the majority, if not all of the costs.

The money you receive as income to cover the running costs of the property should be treated as rent. There are two points to consider with this.

1   If there is no "option to tax" on the property, these rents will be VAT free. The term "option to tax" refers to VAT. When a property is purchased prior to a certain point in time it would be treated as being outside the scope of VAT, and depending on when the property was built or created, after that date it will probably be treated as opted for VAT. This means if it is opted for tax then the rents charged would have to include VAT on the income. This will then increase the rents by 20% (the current rate of VAT).

It is unlikely that any Masonic property has been opted to tax for VAT purposes (as it will raise the rents for no specific purpose), unless the building was recently built from scratch and the land the property is built on had already been "opted to tax". In order to recover the VAT on the build costs, you should obtain specialist advice, as VAT can be a complicated and non-logical tax.

2   With rental income the type of expenditure, which can be offset, and the treatment of losses and surpluses are treated differently to a normal trading business. I will refer to it later, but there are certain types of income, which are treated differently in connection with the costs, and the treatment of losses if applicable. There is one specifically for dealing with property and the corporation tax legislation.

Therefore, if you had significant costs arising from a major repair bill with no element of improvement to the property, then this would give a significant loss for the year in which the repair took place. Consequently, you would have to wait a considerable period to offset this expense.

The reason for this time delay is that a loss in relation to land and property can be offset against other profits from that year, but cannot be carried back to a previous year's profits from property and can only be carried forward to be offset against future years rental income. Therefore, depending upon the magnitude of the repair it will depend on the years taken to offset the loss incurred. It is also likely that over a period this trend will continue to repeat itself.

When a Lodge raises revenue to cover its running costs it is usually done in two ways. The first and most obvious one is rent, and the other is subscriptions. If rents are charged, they may be subject to VAT if the "option to tax" has been exercised. With subscriptions, it depends if the subscription is paid in order to obtain or gain entitlement to any substantial benefit. If so VAT is due on the subscription. It will then form part of the VAT-able turnover as they are treated as VAT-able income (if the entity that owns and runs the property is VAT registered). With the subscriptions fixed as a sum per member, the VAT impact can erode some of the income received. There are certain circumstances in which monies paid can qualify for exemption from VAT. A voluntary donation given when nothing is received in return is not subject to VAT, and is outside the scope of VAT.

Concerning the other income of a Masonic Hall, it is more than likely to be VAT-able, such as the catering and bar sales. If the income exceeds the VAT threshold then you need to register for VAT and account for the VAT on the income. The current VAT registration threshold is £79,000.

However, depending on the level of income from the Masonic Hall, it may be beneficial to de-register for VAT. The current threshold for de-registration is £77,000. It might be worth considering de-registration especially if the Lodge has outsourced the catering to an external caterer and only receives a franchise fee. This has the effect of considerably reducing the VAT-able turnover potential below the de-registration threshold. If your Masonic hall were a regular payer of VAT, it would mean that if you de-registered for VAT this would be the sum you would be better off each year in cash terms. However, you will need to be aware of the rules for de-registration. When a business de-registers for VAT is has to pay back the VAT it has recovered on the assets it has purchased adapted for their current value. Therefore if the current value is such that the output VAT on the disposal is less than £1,000 then you will not be required to repay this output VAT on the de-registration of the assets. The only point, which you will need to consider, would be in reference to any "option to tax" on a property. If an "option to tax" has been made then the VAT on the disposal of the property will be levied. You should ensure you take specific advice concerning the de-registration options and potential implications.

The final point I would make concerning VAT registration is that if the income is above the de-registration threshold, and then it may be worth considering the use of the Flat Rate Scheme for VAT. This is a simplified method of calculating VAT. The way this system works is that an industry specific rate is applied to the Gross Income. Normally a business pays over the difference between the VAT on its Sales (Outputs) and VAT on its Purchases (Inputs). To show the benefits I will work through a small example to illustrate, Table 24.

Table 24

VAT calculated on the standard mechanism		
Gross Vat able sales per annum - Say	120,000	
Output VAT on sales (20/120)		20,000
Gross Vat able purchases per annum - Say	66,000	
Input VAT on purchases (20/120)		11,000
VAT Due to be paid across per annum		9,000
VAT calculated on flat rate mechanism		
Gross Vat able sales per annum - Say	120,000	
Flat rate percentage applied to Public houses - currently 6.5%		7,800
Saving on Flat Rate Scheme calculation		1,200

It will all depend on the specifics of the Masonic Hall, but it may be a benefit to the hall or it may not. You will need to look into the figures to assess the savings, but you must apply the correct flat rate percentage I have illustrated above with the figure used for a Public House to replicate the income streams of a Masonic bar, as this is the nearest sector available. However, with VAT I would always suggest to seek advice before any major decisions are taken or implemented.

Concept of Mutuality

Corporate businesses that trade with a view to making a profit from external connections is a business, which is chargeable to corporation tax. However, the majority of Masonic Lodges trade under the concept of mutuality. This means that all the Lodge subscriptions are collected to pay out the common costs for all. It is not run with a view to making a profit. A surplus may be achieved, but it is never the primary aim. Therefore, the principle of mutuality applies.

The concept of mutuality has been hard fought for many years, as the potential lost revenue to the HMRC has been a cause for concern. It was not until 1955 that the concept was supported by well know case law. The result has been that Masonic Lodges have enjoyed the tax-free benefits of mutual trading since then. The concept does not however apply to all income, and bank interest received and other non-earned income (previously referred to as Schedule D Case III) is still chargeable to Corporation tax at the appropriate rate, which is currently 20% for small company profits below £300,000.

Corporation Tax

Once registered with the HMRC you will need to complete a Corporation tax return form CT600 annually. With effect from the 1st April 2011, all Corporation Tax returns need to be submitted electronically. Prior to this date Lodges enjoyed the luxury of being able to submit the returns by paper. Now the chance of actually getting one submitted by paper is slim to none. The HMRC will write back and say, "Computer says No" in so many words. This electronic submission is now referred to as iXBRL or (inline extensible business reporting language). This requires completion of the form online, which can be done for free on the HMRC website. I do not intend to go through that in this book as it may be only be required by a minimal number of lodges.

The main type of income, which is reported to the HMRC annually on this return, is Bank interest and other investment income received. You can then enter this on the return and pay over the tax at 20% (the current rate of corporation tax) on the interest received. However, if your bank interest has already suffered the deduction of income tax you will need to show the Gross interest received, and then have the corporation tax calculated upon it giving the liability. Then from that liability show, the tax deducted at sources from the bank is shown in Table 25.

Table 25

My Lodge Accounts number XXXX								
Almoners/Charity payments for the year ended 31st December 20XY								
Date	Description	chq number	Total	Almoner expenses & Flowers	Masonic Charities	Master's charity	Masonic Grants paid out	Sundries

The only point with regards to submitting the return is that you need to specify the type of company within the return, and this should be marked as "6 - Members' club or voluntary association - there is special treatment for some types of clubs and associations". You can also specify that there are no accounts due for submission, as you are returning the income from bank interest and mutual trading covers the rest of the earnings. If you are unable to get this to work then you can attach a copy of the accounts as a pdf (Portable Document Format) to the corporation tax return.

If you have other types of income, this will be returned according to the income type. Previously these were all referred to by using the Income tax Schedule References. These references have been in use for many years, and were common forms to accountants, but now the income type refers to the types of income. For example Banks, building society or other interest, and profits and gains from non-trade loan relationships, exchange fluctuations, certain financial instruments and derivative contracts was simply just referred as Schedule D Case III. We all knew what it meant and it was straightforward to accountants, however, the use of calling the income what it actually is means lay people understand it better. If you need any help with the completion of Corporation Tax returns there is a very useful guide available from the HMRC and can be found at www.hmrc.gov.uk/ctsa/ct600-guide-2007.pdf

However, if the tax liability of the Lodge is low, negligible or already taxed at source, then you can apply to the HMRC asking for exemption to complete the tax returns. This should be a formal letter stating the Lodge's Corporation Tax reference number and stating the reasons why you would like to be exempt from returning a corporation tax return each year. Usually if the tax revenue is below £100, they will consider the time and effort in dealing with such returns to be not cost effective.

If you need to register the lodge for the first time, you will need to complete a form notifying the HMRC of the setting up of a new Lodge. The form required is a CT41G (Clubs) and can be downloaded from the HMRC website at www. hmrc.gov.uk/pdfs/ct41g.pdf. You have to register formally the Lodge, as the tax system works on self-assessment, and hence you are responsible if you do not notify them. This means that failure to notify will probably result in a penalty. Once registered, I would then apply for the exemption to complete returns if the tax payable is less than £100. It would definitely be beneficial to apply, as the amount of annual paperwork and reports you will need to complete and submit will be decreased.

Capital Gains Tax

Capital Gains Tax represents the tax liability on assets that are sold for more than they were acquired. As an entity, you will need to include the disposal of the asset and record the gain on the corporation tax return. This will become taxable at the corporation tax rate and will need returning accordingly. If you have applied for an exemption to complete corporation tax returns you will need to notify the HMRC that you have a taxable return to make and complete the appropriate forms. If you do make a disposal of an asset which requires reporting to the HMRC, then you will need to know how much the asset cost, when it was bought and the disposal proceeds (after making due allowance for any selling costs). You will need some specialist help with this as the chargeable gain can be reduced by the use of an indexation allowance on the original cost.

I will not cover it in detail here, but here is a brief example. If you had an asset bought prior to March 1982 and sold in December 2012 then the indexation multiple is 2.107. This means an asset that originally cost say £100,000 sold for £500,000 would have a gain of £400,000, from which the indexation of £210,700 can be deducted. This would give the net gain of £189,300, which would be assessable for tax.

If you are selling a property from which you trade, you can apply for Roll-Over Relief. This effectively means that the gain on a sale of one business asset can be rolled over against the cost of the replacement asset. The rules are relatively complex and an accountant should be contacted concerning the claim for these reliefs. Rollover relief applies to an asset being used by a business replaced by another asset used in the same business. Therefore, for example if you have a Lodge building which is trading, i.e. selling food and bar items, it is trading. However, if it is receiving rent only and the trade is carried out by another mutual organisation then it will not be deemed as trading by the HMRC. Therefore, the relief will not apply. However, there was an extra statutory concession that would have applied in this instance. It was referred to as ESC D15. This has since been withdrawn and replaced by a point of law, and can now be found in the Statutory Instrument 2009/730. This effectively means that you are a non-trading company and do not qualify to use the Rollover relief exemptions. However, you can use the exemptions in connection with a disposal as long as the conditions apply.

I know this works as I received confirmation from the HMRC concerning the disposal and replacement of a Masonic Hall in my Province. This exemption saved hundreds of thousands of pounds. You will need to obtain clearance for any matter prior to the disposal. You can also find more guidance on this in the HMRC tax manuals at http://www.hmrc.gov.uk/manuals/cgmanual/cg60260.htm. With all of the matters in connection with Capital Gains Tax, an accountant should be used, as the individual aspects of each case will need to be considered and as such, the brief outline above cannot cover the many hundreds of pages of tax legislation with which you will need to comply.

Dealing with tax authorities

The ever-increasing reliance on self-assessment by the HMRC also increases your need to complete the returns yourself, and notify the HMRC when any matters change. You need to be aware that as the Treasurer of your Lodge the responsibility will rest with you. The failure to keep the HMRC properly informed will result in penalties being issued. The HMRC are looking at even more ways of raising revenue and if everyone pays on time and completes the right paperwork, they will receive all these monies in order. With any correspondence, please ensure you quote all the correct reference numbers as this helps to track and allocate matters correctly. Above all, the rules will change every year when the respective chancellor delivers the budget, so keep abreast of any changes that are likely to affect your lodge or contact an accountant.

Gift Aid

Gift Aid is only applicable to charities, as this is the tax element of the net contribution towards a charity of a UK taxpayer. Effectively what happens is that for every net contribution of £10 the charity will receive a further £2.50 from the HMRC once the charity has completed and submitted the Gift aid Forms. Tax is worked out, based on the basic rate of tax, which at present is 20%. It is then assumed that the total income is 100% and then the tax is deducted leaving the net figure of 80%. Therefore, the gift aid element is 20% of the 80% or expressed as a fraction ¼ or 25%. Therefore, the 25% of £10.00 is the £2.50, which a qualifying Charity can claim back. This can be used to your own advantage. For example, I have seen Lodges have a collection for either the Provincial or District Charity or even one of the four main Masonic Charities. If this is planned for a particular evening either the Treasurer or the Charity Steward can get in touch with the charity and request gift aid envelopes and pass these amongst the Brethren for completion prior to their donation and collection. Thus increasing the amount of monies paid to the charity by 25%. This way you can increase the charitable giving without increasing the monies actually given. In order to qualify for gift aid the charity has to be registered as a charity with the Charities

Commission and as well as registered with the HMRC. It cannot be done for your own charitable fund collections, as most Lodges do not have a registered charity status as part of their Lodge accounts.

I hope this brief summary has highlighted some of the typical tax areas you may come across as a Lodge Treasurer. However, if any new matter presents itself as an issue and you are unsure how to deal with it, or what the taxation implication will be, given the size and complexity of a particular matter, I would always suggest you seek separate accounting and legal advice to ensure you do not inadvertently cause a financial problem to the Lodge.

AFTERWORD

When I was asked to write this book, it was always my intention to give you a useable guide. When you take on the role of Lodge Treasurer, you will want to make it your own. Personally, I need to know what needs to be done and why. Only then does it become apparent that a change needs to be made. I hope that this book will help you to develop your own conclusions. My thought process was always to provide those simple steps needed for the office of Treasurer. With a bit of luck, I have achieved this and you can now adopt these steps to make the role easier.

I hope that I have successfully dispelled the myth that taking on the role of Lodge Treasurer is for accountants or bank managers and you will not regret being elected to the office. I wish you luck in your appointment. Finally, I would like to say a big thank you to everyone that has helped me in creating this simple guide, and a special thank you to my wife for all the support and understanding during the time it has taken me to write this book.

APPENDIX

Blank Templates for guidance

My Lodge Accounts number XXXX
Members' Register

Names of members	Contact details	Payment type	Date of joining	Brought Forward from previous year	Subs Due for this year	Joining fee	Amount paid	Date paid	Balance out-standing

My Lodge Accounts number XXXX
Main fund receipts for the year 31st December 20XY

Date	Description	Total	Subs 20XY	Subs 20XX	Initi - ation fees	Don - ation	Monies for lodge funds from Events	Stew - ards account	Transfers from savings account	Inte - rest	Sund - ries
		ı	ı	ı	ı	ı	ı	ı	ı	ı	ı

My Lodge Accounts number XXXX
Main fund payments for the year 31st December 20XY

Date	Description	Cheque number	Total	Grand Lodge dues	Provincial Grand Lodge	Lodge rent	Secretarial expenses	Regalia & Ritual expenses	Christmas gratuities	Gifts & Gratuities	Insurance	Sundries	Tyler

My Lodge Accounts number XXXX

Almoners/Charity receipts for the year 31st December 20XY

Date	Description	Total	Alms colle - cted	Donat - ions	Ladies festival	Interest received	Masonic Grants Received	Raffles received
		-	-	-	-	-	-	-

My Lodge Accounts number XXXX

Almoners/Charity payments for the year ended 31st December 20XY

Date	Description	chq number	Total	Almoner expenses & Flowers	Masonic Charities	Master's charity	Masonic Grants paid out	Sundries
			-	-	-	-	-	-

My Lodge Accounts number XXXX

Steward Account & Ladies festival receipts for the year 31st December 20XY

Date	Details	Total	Interest received	Ticket sales	Stewards funds collected	Other income
		-	-	-	-	-

My Lodge Accounts number XXXX

Stewards account and Ladies festival payments for the year ended 31st December 20XY

Date		chq number	Total	Entertain ment costs	Ladies gifts	Flowers	Transfers	Ladies night meal	Festive board costs	Sundries
			-	-	-	-	-	-	-	-

My Lodge Accounts number XXXX

Bank Control accounts for the year ending 31st December 20XY

General lodge account	Current account	Deposit account
Opening balance	-	-
Total receipts	-	-
Total payments	-	-
Closing balance	-	-

	£
Balance per bank statement at 31.12.20XY	-
Add outstanding monies received	-
Deduct payments not yet cleared	-
Closing balance	-

Almoners / Charity Account

Opening balance   -

Receipts   -

Payments   -

Closing balance   -

Balance per Bank statement   -

Difference

Ladies festival account

Opening balance   -

Receipts   -

Payments   -

Closing balance   -

Balance per Bank statement   -

Difference

Grand Charity relief Chest

Opening balance   -

Receipts   -

Payments   -

Closing balance   -

Balance per Bank statement   -

Difference

My Lodge Accounts number XXXX

Projected position for the lodge year 31st December 20XY

Budget

Per Capita fees	Total	Members		Per member
Grand lodge dues	-		=	-
Lodge rent	-	-	=	-
Provincial grand lodge	-	-	=	-
General expenses				
Secretary expenses	-	-	=	-
Ritual & regalia	-	-	=	-
Insurance	-	-	=	-
Tyler fees	-	-	=	-
Sundries	-	-	=	-
Xmas Gratuties and gifts	-	-	=	-

Projected spend per head   -

Current dues	-
estimated spend per head	-
Shortfall per head	-
Shortfall for the year	-

My Lodge Accounts number XXXX
Extended Trial Balance for the year ending 31st December 20XY

	Opening balance		Bank Account 1		Bank Account 2		Bank Account 3		Journals		Income & Expenses		Funds	
	DR	CR	DR	CR	DR	CR	DR	CR	DR	CR	DR	CR	DR	CR
General Account														
Income & expenses														
Income														
Subscriptions														
Initiation fees														
Interest														
Summer BBQ														
Stewards account														
Other receipts														
Sundry receipts														
Donation														
Expenses														
Grand Lodge														
Prov. Grand Lodge														
Lodge rents														
Secretary's Expenses														
Regalia & Ritual														
Christmas/Gratuities														
Gifts & Appeals														
Insurance														
Sundries														
Tyler														
Stewards and Ladies Festival														
Income														
Ticket sales														
Interest received														
Stewards account														
Donation														
Expenses														
Ladies night meal costs														
Festive board costs														
Entertainment costs														
Ladies gifts														
Flowers														
Transfer surplus														
Sundries														
Grand charity relief chest														
Donations received														
Interest received														
Gift aid contribution														

	General fund	Steward's & Ladies Night fund	Grand Relief chest	Almoners fund
Monies paid to Grand lodge	-			
Monies paid to Provincial Grand Lodge	-			
Charity and Almoners account				
Income				
Alm's Collections	-			
Donations	-			
Ladies Festival	-			
Interest	-			
Masonic Grants	-			
Lodge raffle	-			
Expenses				
Almoner + Flowers	-			
Masonic Charities	-			
Other Charities	-			
Provincial Grants	-			
Funds				
General Fund Bank account	-			
General Fund deposit account	-			
Stewards & Ladies festival account	-			
Grand Charity relief chest	-			
Almoners bank account	-			
Almoners funds b/fwd	-			
General fund b/fwd	-			
Ladies Festival fund b/fwd	-			
Grand Charity relief chest fund b/fwd	-			

My Lodge Accounts number XXXX

Summary of Receipts and Payments for the
General Fund for the year ended 31st December 20XY

	20XY		20XX	
	£	£	£	£
Receipts				
Subscriptions		-		-
Initiation fees		-		-
Interest		-		-
Summer BBQ		-		-
Stewards account		-		-
Other receipts		-		-
Sundry receipts		-		-
Donation		-		-
		-		-
Payments				
Grand Lodge	-		-	
Prov. Grand Lodge	-		-	
Lodge rents	-		-	
Secretary's Expenses	-		-	
Regalia & Ritual	-		-	
Christmas/Gratuities	-		-	
Gifts & Appeals	-		-	
Insurance	-		-	
Sundries	-		-	
Tyler	-		-	
		-		-
Excess / (deficit) for the year		-		-

My Lodge Accounts number XXXX

Summary of Receipts and Payments for the
Almoners/Charity Account Fund for the year ended 31st December 20XY

	20XY		20XX	
	£	£	£	£
Receipts				
Alm's Collections	-		-	
Donations	-		-	
Ladies Festival	-		-	
Interest	-		-	
Masonic Grants	-		-	
Lodge raffle	-		-	
		-		-
Payments				
Almoner costs and Flowers	-		-	
Masonic Charities	-		-	
Master's Charity	-		-	
Provincial Grants	-		-	
Sundries	-		-	
		-		-
Excess / (deficit) for the year		-		-

My Lodge Accounts number XXXX

Summary of Receipts and Payments for the
Steward And Ladies Festival Fund for the year ended 31st December 20XY

	20XY		20XX	
	£	£	£	£
Receipts				
Ticket sales		-		-
Interest received		-		-
Stewards account		-		-
Donation		-		-
		_____		_____
		-		-
Payments				
Ladies night meal costs	-		-	
Festive board costs	-		-	
Entertainment costs	-		-	
Ladies gifts	-		-	
Flowers	-		-	
Transfer surplus	-		-	
Sundries	-		-	
	_____		_____	
		-		-
Excess / (deficit) for the year		-		-

My Lodge Accounts number XXXX

Balance sheet
As at 31st December 31st December 20XY

	20XY		20XX	
Current Assets	£	£	£	£
General Fund				
Bank Accounts		-		-
Deposit account		-		-
Almoners/Charity Account		-		-
Ladies Festival & Stewards Account		-		-
Relief Chest Account		-		-
Total Assets		-		-
Represented by:-				
General Fund				
Balance Brought Forward	-		-	
Excess / (deficit) for the year	-		-	
		-		-
Almoners Fund				
Balance Brought Forward	-		-	
Excess / (deficit) for the year	-		-	
		-		-
Ladies Festival				
Balance Brought Forward	-		-	
Excess / (deficit) for the year	-		-	
		-		-
Relief Chest				
Balance Brought Forward	-		-	
Excess / (deficit) for the year	-		-	
		-		-
		-		-

We the undersigned, having been appointed as Auditors of the Lodge, confirm that we have made due enquiry into the books and records maintained by the Treasurer on behalf of the lodge in accordance with Rule 153 of the Book of Constitutions and confirm that the balances held have been duly verified and agreed and that the income and expenditure accounts duly reflect the movements for the lodge funds for the year stated.

....Auditor   ....Auditor

My Lodge Accounts number XXXX

Summary of Receipts and Payments for the
Relief Chest Fund for the year ended 31st December 20XY

	20XY		20XX	
	£	£	£	£
Receipts				
Donations received		-		-
Interest received		-		-
Gift aid contribution		-		-
-				
		-		-
Payments				
Monies paid to Grand lodge	-		-	
Monies paid to Provincial Grand Lodge	-		-	
		-		-
Excess / (deficit) for the year		-		-

BIBLIOGRAPHY

Charities Act 2011

VAT Act 1994

Corporation Taxes Act 2010

Capital Gain Taxes Act 1992

HMRC guidance manuals

UK Statutory Instruments

Book of Constitutions 2013